# Nature and Mortality

# NATURE AND MORTALITY

*recollections of a philosopher in public life*

*Mary Warnock*

**continuum**
LONDON • NEW YORK

**Continuum**

The Tower Building
11 York Road
London SE1 7NX

370 Lexington Avenue
New York
NY 10017–6503

*www.continuumbooks.com*

First published 2003

**British Library Cataloguing-in-Publication Data**
A catalogue record for this book is available from the British Library.

ISBN 0 8264 5940 4

Typeset by YHT Ltd, London
Printed and bound by MPG Books Ltd, Bodmin, Cornwall

# Contents

*Introduction*                                                          1

1  The Education of Handicapped Children and
   Young People                                                         29
2  Human Fertilization and Embryology                                   69
3  Genetics                                                            111
4  Man and Other Animals                                               149
5  Administration of the Arts                                          178

*Index*                                                                223

# Introduction

I have long been an obsessive diary-keeper; and I suppose for ages I had the idea that one day I would write a wonderful autobiography, setting out the truth about what my life had been like. It would be easy, I thought, and a pleasure to do, but a pleasure that could be postponed. After I had written it, what else would there be left to write? I would have said everything true that I knew. However, when at last I thought the time had come to begin, I found that it was impossible. My diaries bored even me; and telling the truth was both difficult and embarrassing.

Besides, I learned that there is an important difference between a diary and an autobiography. A diary, if it is written regularly, is rather like a shopping list. It is in some sense a substitute for memory. Its author writes things down so that he shall not forget them, or at least so that he can in part retrieve them if he does forget. It is true that there is an element of selection in what he writes, but it is a selection quite easily made. The autobiographer, on the other hand, must decide at every step what is and what is not worth writing; and above all, unlike the diarist, he must think of his readership, and the figure he will cut. The diarist does not have to worry about being self-obsessed. Naturally he is, or he would not keep a diary. But nobody likes to be thought of

1

by others as self-obsessed, or indeed uncharitable or boastful. People who write proper autobiographies seem able, some of them, to say things about other people that must offend them or their families; they can boast of their sexual adventures, or reveal their murderous thoughts without shame. I found that in my own case I either did not have the material, or could not bring myself to use it.

So, instead, I wrote a memoir,* more about other people than about me. That does not mean that it was not self-centred. Of course it was, because the people and places I wrote about were all seen from my point of view, with no attempt at impartiality. The book also, I suppose, revealed something about me. Certainly those who reviewed it mostly made the not very bold deduction that I was middle class and had a 'privileged' childhood and education, and from that some deduced that nothing I said could hold much of interest. So why on earth am I embarking again on something approaching autobiography, proper or otherwise?

A distinction is sometimes made between true autobiographies and memoirs. Richard Coe, in his book *When the Grass was Taller: Autobiography and the Experience of Childhood*† wrote this:

> In the great libraries of the world there are significantly fewer volumes of true autobiography than of memoirs. If the isolated self is to be transmuted into something durably significant, it needs to possess a vitality and originality which is very far from common: and it

---

* Mary Warnock, *A Memoir* (London: Duckworth, 2000).
† Richard Coe, *When the Grass was Taller: Autobiography and the Experience of Childhood* (New Haven, CT, and London: Yale University Press, 1985).

needs further to be spurred on by the imperious urge to impart a message or to impart a truth which must not be allowed to vanish, or else by a dose of vanity so strong that never, for one instant, can the author doubt that his own existence in all its intimate and unmomentous detail, is supremely meaningful to the world at large.

There is something in this, but I do not think the distinction can be drawn as clearly as Coe's words suggest. It is rather that there is a continuum between true autobiography and various kinds of memoirs. At the memoir extreme, there are books consisting of a record of events that occurred which could have been compiled equally correctly from official documents. They are held together, it is true, by the fact that they all, or almost all, happened while the same one person was present, or at least was concerned with them, but otherwise they might as well be biography or history. At the other extreme there are autobiographies, often especially of childhood experiences, which aim at an altogether different kind of truth. At the beginning of his autobiography, *The Watcher on the Cast-iron Balcony*,‡ the Australian author Hal Porter wrote, 'Of this house, of what takes place within it until I am six, I alone can tell. That is, perhaps, why I must tell. No one but I will know if a lie be told, therefore I must try for the truth.' And Henry Green, writing his brief autobiography at the outbreak of the Second World War, explained that he wanted to prevent his possessions from becoming muddled; he felt that they must not be wasted. He

---

‡ Hal Porter, *The Watcher on the Cast-iron Balcony* (London: Faber & Faber, 1963).

wanted to take stock of them. His possessions were memories, which were undeniably his. He wrote:

> If I say I remember, as it seems to me I do, one of the maids, that poor thing whose breath smelled, come in one morning to tell us that the *Titanic* had gone down, it may be that much later they had told me I should have remembered, at the age I was then, and that their saying this had suggested I did remember. But I do know, and they would not, that her breath was bad, that when she knelt down to do one up in front it was all one could do to stand there.*

Memory knowledge is a personal possession, but because it is knowledge, it can be passed on. One can 'share' it, as they say these days. It can become part of history, and thus, according to Thucydides a possession for all time, a κτημα εἰς ἀει.

And so I have the feeling that I want to take stock of some of my memory knowledge, specifically concerned with the problems in public policy with which I have been engaged from time to time. Reports of committees of inquiry get published, and although they may be read, perhaps accepted, and incorporated in legislation, or become part of the background of continuing controversy, and although some, such as the Robbins Report on university provision (1963), or the Plowden Report on primary school education (1967), have been extremely influential, what is not known, except to those who participated, is the series of events leading up to the publication of the reports. It may seem easy to have come out with the conclusions and the recommendations. I

---

* Henry Green, *Pack My Bag* (London: Hogarth Press, 1940), p. 8.

want, in what follows, to record some of the hurdles that had to be overcome before the final report appeared, the arguments that had to be examined, the often ludicrous obstacles to progress that seemed to spring up like partridges in the path of the committee, and the sometimes crucial influence of individual members of the committee. I would love to know more about the story of the conclusions reached by both those educational committees I have mentioned, especially the Plowden Committee. Bridget Plowden told me, when she was chairman of the Independent Broadcasting Authority (IBA), and I a member, that she 'couldn't write', and so she got a young sociologist, Maurice Kogan, to do the drafting. Good a writer as Kogan has since proved himself to be, I could not imagine doing such a thing. And then the volatile and brilliant philosopher A. J. Ayer was a member of the committee, totally ignorant of maintained school education, exceedingly prone to boredom, and a highly theoretical egalitarian. I would love to know in detail what he contributed to the deliberations. It is not that I think people learn from other people's mistakes and avoid repeating them; indeed I think that mistakes are inevitable in attempts to settle questions of what should be public policy. Nothing is so difficult as trying to be a good utilitarian and foresee the consequences of a particular recommendation within an uncertain and unending future. It is rather that the narrative of how conclusions were reached may perhaps have a certain intrinsic curiosity value.

There was another, more personal reason why I decided that I wanted now, at what by any reckoning must be the last stage of my life, to record what I could of my memory knowledge. I wanted to analyse it, and try to find out what motivated me to do the things I have done. Geoffrey, my husband, who knew me well (all too well, I sometimes thought), used to remark that I would say 'yes' to anything. But this was not an explanation, more a statement of fact. Sometimes he would quote from Hobbes and say that I was engaged in a 'reckless pursuit of power after power'. There was truth in this; but then I think it is true of everyone. No one likes to be someone else's slave. Whatever the sphere of activity, one likes to be in control of it. This is why these days domestic service is thought of as intolerable. In the days of great Victorian or Edwardian households, within each sphere – the kitchen, the pantry, the wine-cellar or the garden – one could rise up to take control, and in each of these areas of activity someone would be in charge and exercise power. Now that such hierarchies no longer exist there is no power to be exercised in domestic service, and therefore it is despised. I certainly liked to feel that I was in control domestically, of how the children were brought up, of what we had to eat, of how life was generally arranged. And professionally I liked to feel that I had control over how I taught, and the hours within which I worked. When I felt that control was slipping, I fell into panic. But I believe that this is the common lot. I was by no means extraordinary.

There was at least one occasion, I must admit, when I said 'yes' just for the sake of it, and this was when I was asked whether I would allow my name to go forward for the election of Mistress of Girton. This was in 1984. Twelve years earlier I had left the Oxford High School, and since that time I had held a variety of positions in Oxford: research fellowships at Lady Margaret Hall and St Hugh's, and lecturerships at Balliol, then Somerville, then Christ Church (which was by far the most enjoyable; but the person I was standing in for was ending his stint as Senior Censor, and my term of office was in any case coming to an end). But

I had never had what I considered a proper job. I thought I would like to have a simple answer to the question 'What do you do?', and a simple way of describing myself at the bottom of articles and reviews, rather than 'formerly' this that or the other. Besides, it was nice to be considered for a job at the age of sixty, exactly when I would have had to retire if I had remained a schoolmistress. Also, this was the second time I had been asked to stand for Girton (the first occasion, four or five years earlier, was just when Geoffrey began his term as Vice-Chancellor, and I was not even remotely tempted to consider it). This time, it felt like destiny.

These were all frivolous reasons. I certainly knew well enough, being married to one, that becoming Head of House in Oxford or Cambridge would not give one power. All the same, when I went to be interviewed, no one asked me whether if offered the job I would accept it, and as I came away I was fairly sure that I did not want it. The interviews seemed to have gone disastrously badly. At the full meeting of the Governing Body I discovered what I later confirmed, that the acoustics in the Stanley Library where meetings were held were appalling, and I could hardly hear a word that was said at the far end of the table. In particular I could not hear the economics fellow, Frank Wilkinson, who always spoke with his hand over his mouth, as if to keep back hostile words that might issue across the barrier of his teeth. He, though I later came to like him, was my manifest enemy, a class enemy, I felt, for he had views that were, from my perspective, very far to the left.

I put forward all kinds of fancy ideas about how Girton ought to lead the field in collaboration with schools over admissions policy, agreeing to accept candidates with mixed-subject A levels, or A levels of lower grades, if they had been at schools where they had been badly taught, or had a disadvantaged background (all of which ideas seem amazingly fashionable now, but in any case were inappropriate to try to sell to Girton, which had a wider range of undergraduates from socially deprived areas than almost any Cambridge college). These ideas were not well received, and I had the strong impression that I had put my foot in it.

After the formal interview, I sat alone in the grand surroundings of the Mistress's study, waiting for individual fellows to come to talk to me. Two came. One was the then librarian, a completely dotty person who was soon to leave; the other an extremely nice fellow in modern languages. For some reason we fell to talking about the Perse School in Cambridge, where she had been a pupil, and it soon became clear that we had both been in love with the same Latin teacher, who had moved on from Winchester to Cambridge soon after the outbreak of war. So from then on we recalled the elegance and charm of Miss Genochio, and talked of nothing else. Then I was told that two other fellows who had been on holiday together in Scotland wished to see me the following morning at eleven o'clock. I had planned to drive home that evening, so I was not pleased to have to stay the night. But I did stay, and slept not one single wink because of going over the disastrous interview of the day before. When it came to talking to the two fellows, a zoologist and a botanist, who did everything together, and whom I afterwards always greatly liked and admired, it turned out that they had been staying at Achiltibuie in Wester Ross, a place I knew and loved. So we spent an hour talking about that, and then I was allowed home. I was therefore disconcerted when, later that day, the Vice-Mistress rang up to say that the flag was flying for the new Mistress and that I had been elected. I had genuinely thought I would have time to think it over. I believe that even at that late stage I should have withdrawn.

# Introduction

There were some things about Cambridge that I loved. I loved my huge flat in college, though it was in some ways the least comfortable place I have ever lived in. It was built by a Cambridge architect, David Robertson, who had a passion for concrete and glass. He had been responsible for some new buildings at New College, Oxford, and also for the new undergraduate block at St Hugh's when I was both a fellow, and for a time Estates Bursar, responsible for the buildings. So I knew his style, and recognized it at once when I first saw the flat. It was brutal from the outside, sticking out like every kind of carbuncle from the dark Victorian brick of the rest of the college; and inside, the fireplace in the drawing-room was a huge concrete object taking up the whole of one wall; another two walls were made entirely of glass. This meant that when it rained, or the wind blew, the whole flat seemed to shudder like a ship in a storm; draughts whistled round, and even with a fire and central heating the only way to survive was to be wrapped in an eiderdown. On the other hand, when the sun shone the flat was like a greenhouse, which was even more difficult to deal with. All the same, I loved having so much space, and being able to play my record-player as loud as I liked. It was a wonderful place for entertaining, whether of twenty or so undergraduates, or of friends who came to stay. Geoffrey loved it, too, and after he retired he used to come as often as he could, especially to help me out at guest-nights. He was much better than I was at talking to people he didn't know, or didn't want to talk to. Years of dining in hall at Hertford, 'with the troops' as he said, had made him an expert. And the ex-Vice Chancellor of Oxford was a smart co-host. So I benefited greatly from his presence, and from the familiar pleasure of 'going over' a party after it was finished.

I greatly liked talking to undergraduates as well, whether at the parties I gave or when they came to see me by themselves, or even when making speeches on formal occasions, when I would enjoin them to think of themselves as Girtonians for ever, once they had joined the college. After one such rhetorical triumph, a sweet classical scholar from Belfast came to tell me that he had made his will, and left everything to Girton. He was about to start a career as a keeper in a provincial museum, so I did not place much hope on his benefaction. But I was tremendously touched.

All the same, in spite of these and other pleasures, it was difficult living in Cambridge during the week and going home at weekends and for as much of the vacation as I could. I made no friends; I never once went to anyone's house. If I was entertained, as I was a lot, it was always in a college, often at one of the dire Cambridge college feasts, which seemed so much longer and more formal than any guest-nights in Oxford. My greatest friend was my secretary, with whom I gossiped endlessly (she enjoyed talking about her colleagues, and I never liked to think what she might have told other people about me), and who always helped me with my undergraduate parties as well as typing the books or articles that I wrote. And one sad thing was that I no longer took pleasure in what little teaching I did. This was a change, because especially in the last four years when I had been a lecturer at Christ Church I had enjoyed teaching enormously. (The only other time that I had not enjoyed it was in the early 1970s when I was a lecturer at Balliol, and my pupils were all extremely disaffected and critical of the syllabus, wanting to study nothing but Marxism in various forms.)

The problem was really that I felt no confidence in my ability to teach philosophy in Cambridge. At Oxford no one can read philosophy without doing, in equal measure, one or even two other subjects. There I knew exactly how to gauge the amount of work to give my students, taking into account whether they were truly interested in philosophy as opposed to the other subject they were doing, but always on the look-out for their becoming more interested than they had been, and so needing a longer reading list. I also knew, after years of trial and error, what was the best order in which to take the topics to be covered, and what lectures I thought they really must go to. It takes years to learn this kind of thing. But in Cambridge, where students reading philosophy do nothing else, I felt at sea. Surely they ought to be doing more advanced work than their Oxford contemporaries, having twice as much time to devote to it? Surely I ought to be treating them more as I would treat B.Phil philosophers in Oxford, and expect them, up to a point, independently to pursue the subjects that had come to interest them? Yet they never seemed to know more than their Oxford counterparts, and they were a lot worse at handing in essays on time. Perhaps I never taught any one who was much good; but at any rate I felt that I was failing them.

There was one pupil I really failed. She had come from overseas, though she now lived in England with her family. I have no recollection of interviewing her when she applied to the college, but I suppose I must have, since I was always given a hand in selecting people to read philosophy. I know that she came up full of enthusiasm; and she was also a Wimbledon-standard tennis player. When I taught her she was in her last year. She was living out of college, sharing a flat with friends. She seemed to have no interest in philo-sophy, and she found writing an essay extremely difficult, let alone handing it in on schedule. I tried to find out how she spent her time, but she was not forthcoming, except to say that she had given up tennis. I asked her vaguely if she had any worries, as well as whether she had any plans for the next year. But the fact was that I saw her so little, and received so many notes and telephone calls postponing her supervisions, that I had little chance to talk to her, and simply found her frustrating. Then one week, following a much better supervision than was usual, for which she had written a decent essay on which I could congratulate her, I got a note from her asking to see me again, because she wanted to go further into a question about Hume that had come up in her supervision. I was delighted. I thought it was a breakthrough, and that, as she still had two more terms before her tripos examinations, we might at last make some progress.

The day before she was due to come back, I had to go a long distance from Cambridge to take part in a conference at some school. While I was there, I was summoned to the telephone and told that she had committed suicide, having been found in her flat by her friends. I felt the most appalling guilt. How could I possibly have missed the signs of depression? Her inability to get work done on time, her vague inattention, to say nothing of her having given up tennis, which she had loved, should have told me that she was in trouble, but I had done nothing except feel irritation. I blamed myself bitterly. I had seen more of her than anyone else, in the past term, apart from her contemporaries, and I had failed to help her. It was not as if I was ignorant of depression. A great friend of mine from schooldays (whose mother had committed suicide while we were still at school) had been a manic-depressive, and soon after we got married Geoffrey and I looked after her, and her children, as best we could for a long time, with Geoffrey, who loved her dearly, being better than I was at allowing her to do absolutely nothing if that was what she felt like. He was temperamentally more sympathetic to depression than I. And I had had pupils in Oxford who suffered from depression. My blindness was inexcusable.

I went to see her parents in London, and they told me that she had had severe depression before she left school, but had recovered. They showed me a diary that her friends had found in the flat. It made terrible reading. She referred constantly to 'the pit' which she knew lay before her, and into which she finally fell. She said she knew she would never be able to climb out if she went down to the bottom. I wish, of course, that we had known before she came up to Girton that she had had clinical depression. At least we would have been on the alert. But the problem of medical confidentiality is acute, and I have never known how best to solve it. Perhaps, as we get more accustomed to the genetic component in such conditions as schizophrenia, we shall also get better at deciding what should and should not be revealed to those who are charged with looking after people like my Greek pupil. Her parents behaved extraordinarily well and generously, and came with their other daughter to the memorial service we had in chapel, with music which her friends arranged, and the college choir sang. It was terribly moving. I find suicide among adolescents and young adults intolerable to think about, far worse even than the deaths of those of the same age by disease or accident. I do not think that university life actually causes such suicides; but it is possible to feel extremely isolated at university, where the anxiety produced not necessarily by the thought of examinations (though this may be acute) but by the effort to keep up a steady flow of work, for which you and you alone are responsible, may be a factor leading to suicide among those prone to depression.

This, anyway, was my worst experience in Cambridge. One way and another I was glad to leave, though grateful to Girton for having appointed me. But, as I have said, it was probably an occasion on which I should for once have said 'no'.

Girton apart, I think what motivated me to accept membership or chairmanship of government and other committees of inquiry has been the pleasure of having new topics presented to me which I knew at a theoretical level would be interesting, although I was ignorant of them. And the pleasure was enhanced by the further knowledge that the discussions of these topics would not be merely theoretical, like discussions in a philosophical tutorial, but would have to be refined into recommendations, which might actually have some influence on what happened next. So the pursuit was not so much of power as of possible influence, along with a desire to discover something about new subjects. Of course it would have been possible to find out about new things by reading for a degree at the Open University, and these days I often consider doing so. But I very much doubt if I would ever have the persistence or determination to keep going through the whole course. The great advantage of committees such as those on which I have served is that they not only opened new horizons but also kept one at it. Having agreed to become a member, one could not default.

Enjoying the kind of work that such committees involve is, I believe, a form of mental laziness. This seems a surprising analysis at first sight. But I believe it is right in a quite important way. It keeps one busy, while relieving one from the necessity of setting one's own agenda. For people like me who enjoy thinking, but who are entirely unoriginal thinkers, it is ideal, more akin, perhaps, to translating than to writing a new book. The aim is to get things right, if possible lucidly and elegantly, but what is to be got right is, as it were, given. Somebody else had set one the problem. This exactly suits my cast of mind. No wonder I was an efficient undergraduate, turning out essays on a variety of subjects, putting away one lot of books and getting out the next.

But the question may still be raised of whether I was any good at the work, even if it suited me. I think I was, and am, a quite good member of committees. I do not either sit in silence or talk too much (at least not very often); I never talk to my neighbours (something that I regard as an unforgivable fault in committee members), and I do not try to raise again a question that has been settled. As a chairman, I do not quite know what marks to award myself. In some ways I think I was quite good, in that I was not too solemn, and indeed aimed to make the members laugh, if it was at all possible. I had a reasonable determination to get things done in time, and turn out reports when required, and I positively enjoyed drafting, about which I was extremely bossy. But I am not altogether decisive; and this is why whether or not I am at a lowly level power-hungry, I know that I could never manage if I had to exercise serious power, as a chairman of a big company, or a senior minister with a spending department. I would think I knew, as I lay awake in the night, that I had made the wrong decision, but in the morning I would think that after all I had been right; and I would swing backwards and forwards between alternatives in a hopelessly obsessional way. I enormously admire people who are decisive, even if they sometimes get things wrong; but I am certainly not one of them.

It is sometimes assumed that when you have been working on a committee which has finally brought out its report, the subject matter must have become and must remain a prevailing interest in your life. Fortunately this is not so, otherwise I, for one, would be burdened with a number of very strange passions, such as infanticide, dangerous dogs, euthanasia and the organization of medical education. In fact, and here again there is an analogy with undergraduate essays, it is easy to forget all about the subjects that have been temporarily your preoccupation after the work is done, but there is not, as there is for undergraduates, the painful necessity of revising them all again for a final examination.

There were two subjects, however, which had always been of interest to me, and where what I learned from the committee work I did had a lasting effect on the way I thought about them. The first was the work that I did as chairman of the Committee of Inquiry into the Education of Children with special needs, which reported in 1978, having sat for four years. I have described the life of this committee and our report at some length in Chapter 1, and so will say no more about it here, except that what I valued about it, for my own part, was not so much its particular focus on 'special needs' as the necessity our deliberations imposed on us of constantly bearing in mind the question of what schools were for, and how they could better fulfil their proper function of providing education for all their pupils, whatever their abilities. Though I had everything to learn about specific disabilities and learning difficulties, I had always been fascinated by the question of what makes a good school; and this became part of our field of inquiry.

When I took my first real teaching job, at Sherborne School for Girls in 1944, between Mods and Greats at Oxford, I immediately knew that I was at a good school; and I wanted to analyse what was good about it. (The answer, in this case, was obvious: it had a charismatic head, H. V. Stuart, a Great Headmistress if ever there was one.) Ever since then I have regarded schools as important. It is not only that children spend so many hours at school, but that their hours are spent at an age when they are still capable of change, of being, if not moulded, then at least influenced, for good or ill, by their teachers and their environment. I strongly agree with Aristotle both that we are partly

16

was born – though by all accounts he was an eccentric and rather lazy schoolmaster, who entered the profession fairly late in life, and only ever taught in one school, Winchester. But at least he did not think himself above school; he took it seriously. I still get an enormous sense of excitement and a perception of widening of horizons when I go to what is manifestly a good school. For example, in the late 1980s I spent a day taking part in a television documentary in Hanwell Primary School where David Winkley (now Sir David) was headmaster. We started with assembly (only half the school could fit into the hall at a time, so another assembly had to be held later). I shall not forget the march in of the children to a recording of music by Monteverdi, and then the silent sitting on the floor, cross-legged, of what seemed to me like a sea of black and brown children, with a few white faces among them. David Winkley was standing up, a piano behind him. Somehow he managed to play the piano and still face the children, and after a reading and a short question-and-answer session about what they meant by the word 'peace', he got them singing. The first time through he said 'that was good; but I think you could do better'. The second time through was thrilling. I came away trembling with the sound, and the enthusiasm and discipline in this school. It sent shivers down my spine, as did reading some of the poems written by pupils from his lunch-time writers' class, which he taught himself, and which was for the most advanced Year 6 pupils who had been picked out for their special ability (there were also classes for advanced mathematicians, as well as numerous support groups for slow readers, and others with special needs). It was the most truly wonderful school, and I wonder what the legislation going through parliament at the present time which will give permission to selected schools to 'innovate' would make of it, a place where innovation was what David Winkley was doing, day by day, without benefit of legislation, and often in the face of fierce opposition from the local education authority.

I am inclined to think, now all is more or less said and done, that I would have done better (by which I mean, I suppose, that I would have been happier) if I had stayed with school-teaching all my life. I like talking to children. And I certainly never tire of hearing the sagas, dramas, disasters and triumphs that make up life in the school, Dulwich College, where my youngest daughter teaches. Through her good offices, I spent a morning at Dulwich not long ago, taking two assemblies, and then spending a morning teaching, philosophy I suppose, to various classes of different ages. I had forgotten the excitement and demands of teaching a class of perhaps 24 children, all keen to contribute, all eager to absorb new ideas, all articulate and confident. I ended my morning, exhausted but exhilarated, thinking 'if I had my life again, this and only this is what I would do.' Who knows?

The second topic which has, as it were, spilled over from the public arena of committees into private life is what may roughly be called nature. I will try to make clear what I mean by this word, but the process will not be altogether straightforward. From 1979 until 1986 I was a member of a standing Royal Commission on Environmental Pollution. This was an enormously enjoyable committee, chaired, in my time, first by a biochemist from Cambridge, Hans Kornberg, later Master of Christ's College, and then by a chemist from Oxford, Dick Southwood, the next Vice-Chancellor but one after Geoffrey. Both of them were in their different ways genial and amusing chairmen, both equally savage in their dealings with the civil servants who were called to give evidence from the then Ministry of Agriculture and Fisheries (MAFF), as inept then as they were in 2001 in their dealings with the foot-and-mouth epidemic (and the Ministry has now been abolished). The members of the Commission were mostly scientists, and the secretary was a scientist, but there were a few 'lay' members, an economist, a lawyer, a medical professor concerned with public health, and me, the philosopher. Our discussions were like an idealized high table or common room conversation in an Oxford or Cambridge college, where everyone joined in, everyone got on with everyone else without plotting or jealousy, and there were no factions, no split between arts and science. (It is an ideal seldom if ever attained in real colleges, where college politics, long-held grudges, ineradicable antipathies, awkward guests and the anxieties and frustrations of daily life make general conversation almost impossible.)

The Royal Commission generally took a topic and examined it for eighteen months or two years, and then brought out a report. When I joined, a report on the disposal of nuclear waste had just been published, and we were moving on to oil pollution. We then tackled petrol fumes, and in my last year we looked superficially at a variety of subjects, such as chemical waste and river pollution, to see which next merited an in-depth examination. Oil pollution was, for me, the most interesting. It also involved the most travel, including a visit to the Shetlands, where we saw sheep grazing happily and apparently flourishing on a diet of seaweed on the shore, and we could look at the puffins and guillemots and other birds whose lives were threatened by oil slicks out to sea. We also went by helicopter to land on an oil rig in thick fog, where we were given the most magnificent lunch, before being shown over the working parts, and I had to try to conceal my terror at climbing up and down slippery ladders out over the sea, where falling would have meant certain death. On the way back from this trip our pilot was summoned by radio to another rig, some 50 miles further out to sea, where we had to go to pick up a crew member who had broken his leg. There was still dense fog, and for the second time we experienced the miracle of hovering over a rig which had been invisible until a moment before, and then landing neatly on a space that looked no bigger than a pocket-handkerchief.

We stayed in Lerwick for several days, talking to oil people, fishermen and farmers, and to the local government officials who did not like our enquiries at all, and who refused to talk to us unless we sat through one of their meetings, which we were obliged to do, though we could not understand one word of what was being said. Even Hans Kornberg's usually irrepressible puns and jokes dried up after this occasion. Apart from that meeting, it was enormously educative. I was becoming learned about the chemical properties of oil, and about booms and foam and other means of attempting to limit the damage of spillages; but most of all I was beginning to raise questions about pollution in general, and to ask why we value a clean coastline, with its marine and offshore fauna, so highly. It was the first time I had seriously considered whether 'the environment' or 'nature' is valued intrinsically, for its own sake, or for the sake of some other more obviously human value, as a 'utility', or for its contribution to human well-being.

I found that some of my scientific colleagues, a rather Spartan and unsentimental marine biologist for example, did not mind if all the puffins abandoned Sumborough Head and the offshore waters of Shetland, arguing that they were not an endangered species, and would simply find another habitat to suit them, in Iceland for example. (Indeed I was astonished when, some ten years later, I visited Iceland, and found that I was offered puffin for dinner. They were prized as a welcome, though to me not very noticeable, change from fish, and were certainly not in short supply.) This rational man argued that biodiversity was something to be valued for the sake of the general continuation of life on earth, and therefore species should be conserved as long as possible, even though it could not be for ever; but that it did not matter where in the world the species existed. He was a thoroughgoing Darwinian, capable of thinking dispassionately about a time when life had not appeared on the planet, and about a distant future when it would have disappeared again. He looked at this prospect, and did not flinch from it. It was then that I realized how sentimental my reactions were. I wanted the puffins to remain there, at Sumborough Head, where they belonged and could be seen by people like me.

Equally, I found it difficult to agree with the economist who argued that a clean coastline was an amenity to which a precise economic value could be attached. Clearing the beaches of the traces of an oil-spill could on this view be judged worthwhile or not on the basis of a strict cost–benefit calculation. The cost would be the resources needed for setting up booms and barriers, and for actually clearing the oil from the beaches, as well as for keeping permanent policing in place to stop the deliberate release of oil from ships too close inshore, all of which could be reasonably accurately assessed. The benefit would be income from the tourist trade, not only from those who would wish to sit on clean beaches and swim in clean sea (though there would be little of either in the Shetlands, one might think), but from those who wished to pursue their ornithological or geological interests. Based on such a calculation, the economist was inclined to think that cleaning up the Shetlands was too expensive to be justified.

But whether this was so or not, to think of the coastline of the Shetlands as an 'amenity' seemed to me to diminish its value, and even to imply a contradiction. An amenity is something like a park, a zoo or a cinema, a man-made item, deliberately designed to give pleasure or amusement to those who will visit it. If the amenity is out of doors, one can immediately envisage the car parks, the lavatories, the judiciously placed seats for the aged to rest on, the gift-shop and the finger-posts. And thus the paradox of nature is revealed.

Since the birth of the Romantic movement we have learned and not forgotten Rousseau's lesson that what comes from God is good and beautiful, but that man corrupts it by his interventions. Rousseau notoriously applied this belief to the education of children. But it had an even more potent effect on nineteenth-century attitudes towards nature, attitudes which most of us have not shaken off, and would not altogether want to, even if we could. Many of our deepest imaginative pleasures and aesthetic insights come to us through the medium of nature. But these attitudes have become more and more complicated.

First, there is the obvious, but none the less striking difference between, let us say, Dr Johnson and Wordsworth: in the eighteenth century, nature was still more or less divided between the wild and the cultivated, of which the cultivated was much to be preferred. Travellers, even travellers in the United Kingdom, generally found mountainous country, for example, dangerous and ugly. Johnson, on his tour to the Western Isles of Scotland with Boswell, wrote in his journal, 'an eye accustomed to flowery pasture and waving harvests is astonished and repelled by this wide extent of hopeless sterility'. And, also in the eighteenth century, John Morton wrote, in a guidebook to his own county of North-amptonshire, that 'here are no naked and craggy rocks, no rugged and unsightly mountains or vast solitary woods to dampen and intercept the view'. The change in sensibility from this to the romantic yearning for wilderness is vast. And we, most of us, have the hankering for wilderness not far below the surface. This of course easily becomes a kind of snobbishness, such as mine over the concept of 'amen-ities'. I want to go to the West Highlands, or indeed to Shetland, but I do not want everyone else in the world to go there with me. I want to be alone with my precious sensi-bilities and my openness to 'thoughts that do often lie too deep for tears'. How can I experience them, if a lot of ramblers with the 'right to roam' come trampling up my mountain path, especially if they demand a car park and a lavatory and a seat for granny in the Picnic Area?

And there are other kinds of human intervention in the sacred Garden of Eden that we call nature which we may deplore and resent. In an article written in 1998, a Cam-bridgeshire farmer, Robin Page, passionately inveighed against the new industrialized farming in his own county. 'The truth is that over the years our farms have been turned into factories and the land has been transformed into fea-tureless fields – the factory floor.' He went on to say, 'I do not need an environmentalist to tell me about the decline in farmland birds or inform me of the skylarks' diminishing song. They have been obvious to me for years.' I owe this quotation to Professor David Wiggins. Here natural beauty and a diversity of wildlife have been sacrificed to agricultural profitability, and the eighteenth-century ideal of cultivation has turned sour and horrible.

## Introduction

I began to learn from thinking about nature as I did in my days on the Royal Commission that the natural world is to be valued for its own sake, and at every turn human beings have an obligation to remember this value along with others, and to try to balance what is in the interests of the natural world against what is specifically in the interests of some group of humans, such as farmers or ramblers. The Judaeo-Christian idea of stewardship of nature is a powerful metaphor. To say this is not to say much, but it is perhaps worth saying all the same, because it is often assumed, especially by economists, that no interest can trump commercial or other financial interests, and that concepts such as welfare must in the end be translatable into terms of wealth. The difficulty is that while most people could agree that poverty is the enemy of welfare, it is far less clear what is the opposite of poverty. It may not be wealth, but something more like 'having enough', or 'not suffering deprivation'. That is to say, everyone can see that real poverty is a cause of suffering, including disease, crime and lack of hope; but the duty to attempt to rescue people from poverty does not necessarily entail a duty to make them wealthy or even to encourage them to make themselves wealthy, if this is at the expense of other things that society values, such as the existence of skylarks in Cambridgeshire. I suppose that Green politics attempts to introduce the recognition that the natural world is to be valued for itself, and not simply as a means of production, and this, though it seems obvious enough to individuals who gain comfort or inspiration from the romantic contemplation of nature, is not an easy idea to incorporate into social or other public policy.

To add to the complexities of the idea of the natural, there is another sort of human intervention which is held by many to corrupt and ruin the works of God, and that is biotechnology, and in particular the genetic modification of crops and animals, including human animals. The objection to these developments is often couched in terms of their being 'contrary to nature' or simply 'unnatural'. The committee that I chaired on human fertilization and embryology came right at the beginning of the biotechnology age, or so it now seems, and at the time I, certainly, and even a biologist, could not have foreseen the kinds of things that are happening now in the biological and medical sciences. So here again I have had to attempt to understand what we mean by 'the natural' in this context, and once more to come to the cautious conclusion that we must try to see human intervention at a genetic level as an advance in medical procedures which can perhaps one day offer us huge benefits in providing ways to remedy conditions for which there is now no cure, such as Parkinson's disease; but that we must not be too confident, or too careless of what we regard as the natural order. I certainly do not hold that, in general, medical interventions can be condemned as being 'against nature'; nor do I see anything preferable in so-called natural remedies for disease over those that are either chemical or surgical. What works is good, as far as medicine goes, or so it seems to me. There is, however, one thought that alarms me, and that is the possibility, however remote, that scientists may one day discover a means of renewing the cells in the human body one by one as they begin to wear out, thus indefinitely postponing death.

Of course there would be huge practical problems that would result from putting such a scheme into effect on any large scale. There would be simply too many people in the world, and too many people holding down good jobs and preventing others from rising to the top. In any case, only the rich could afford to have the cell-renewal operations, and the rest would be left to die. There could be no greater injustice. Nevertheless, these considerations apart, I believe that the indefinite postponement of death would be flying in the face of nature in a way that would change all our beliefs about ourselves, and the meaning of our lives. It is perhaps easiest to couch such fears in the terms of religion. To make ourselves immortal would be to makes ourselves gods. But without having recourse to mythology, I believe that, as things are, when we know that we, like all other animals and plants, will one day die, our lives have a shape, a point which they could not have if they could go on virtually for ever.

Moreover, one of the things that constantly gives significance both to our own life and the lives of other people whom we love or admire is that there is a contrast, sometimes a conflict, between what, being mortal and having a more or less precarious or fragile hold on life, we can actually do, and what we can aspire to or imagine. The creative imagination, it seems to me, feeds on this contrast, allowing us to grasp, or partly grasp, what is beautiful or what is tragic or what is in some other way inspirational. Being mortal, we know that there is an urgency in our lives. We have not got all the time in the world, only the little time that is ours. In this sense we are part of a world of mortal creatures, and can feel ourselves to be so. And we can feel, as well, the proper distance that there is between the ephemeral and the everlasting. One central part of our idea of nature is that it can do without us; the earth will continue to exist when we are no longer there, as it existed before we were born. So mortality is the foundation on which we build all our perceptions and our emotions, whether expressed in literature, art, music or religion. The ideas of nature and mortality coexist and have equal weight. I would not want to see them torn apart. But, despite these gloomy fears, being

27

a perpetual optimist, I do not believe that these terrible changes will come about – not, at least, in my lifetime. And that is one of the comforts of dying.

And so, in the book that I have rashly written, there is a partly narrative thread. I did this, that and the other. But there is partly a thread that is like the 'recreations' entry in *Who's Who*, where my entry used to list gardening, music and golf. I cut out golf after Geoffrey died. I loved playing (and still love watching it on television), but was so bad a player that I would have been ashamed to play with anyone except him. I have spared my readers gardening. Gardeners do not bore other gardeners, but they bore everyone else. The thread that I hope will become clear in the course of the chapters that follow is that of the issues of public policy which have been particularly important to this particular public servant: education, nature and art. And in the idea of nature, I naturally include that of human nature, in all its gossip-worthy details.

# 1 The Education of Handicapped Children and Young People

Early in 1974, while the Conservative government was still in office, I was asked by the Secretary of State for Education, Margaret Thatcher, whether I would chair a committee of inquiry into the education of the handicapped. Of course I said I would, rashly, but I'm afraid characteristically, undeterred by my total lack of knowledge of the subject, or indeed interest in it. After the defeat of the Tories in the general election of that year I assumed that I should hear no more of the committee; but in fact the Labour government decided to go on with it, and so I was committed.

I did not immediately realize what fundamental issues would be raised by this inquiry. Though I myself have always been, both professionally and emotionally, involved in education, I recognize that, compared with, say, foreign policy, or law and order, it is not thought of as a particularly important, let alone prestigious subject. Though, to his credit, Tony Blair put education at the top of his agenda in 1997, the perception of education as in some degree dowdy has not greatly changed. This incidentally, in my view, accounts for the low pay and low status of teachers in society. In the eyes of many powerful and successful people, education is something everybody goes through, and can then forget, like adolescence. Yet the place of education in society is of the greatest possible significance. Providing a proper, liberating education for everybody is the key to social justice. Society divides itself between the educated and the uneducated; and unless some attempt is made to provide education for those who are likely to slip through the educational net, the gap will inevitably widen. This became clear to me as time went on, though not, I'm afraid, clear enough. In the background of the whole inquiry was the thought of the vast numbers of children who, without suffering any identifiable impairment, nevertheless fail to engage at all with education, because they are alienated from it by poverty, violence or hostility to 'the system'.

Another crucial question to arise was the scope of the concept of education itself. In the past a distinction had been drawn between 'education' and 'training'. It had been assumed that education was broadly speaking intellectual, a matter of enabling people to understand things, while training was a matter of causing people to do things, whether they understood what they were doing or not. Dogs and horses could be trained, as well as humans. Such a distinction is based on an outdated faculty psychology, according to which reason, the distinctive mark of humanity, could be separated conceptually from other faculties, and educated almost in isolation. The committee had inevitably to rethink this assumption; the distinction between education and training simply withered away. The function of teachers is to help people to learn; and there are innumerable things to learn and ways of learning them.

Finally, as time went on, I at least became more and more aware of the acute difficulty of getting members of different professions to take one another seriously. Again creditably, New Labour put what it jokily called 'joined-up thinking' high on its agenda, and made genuine efforts to get one government department to talk to another. Whether there has been any progress I cannot say. All I know is that I, in ignorance, was amazed at the degree to which doctors wash their hands of questions about education when they diagnose a baby born with sensory or intellectual impairment; and at the degree, even more astonishing, to which social workers fail to recognize that education is the only way through which their clients can climb out of their prison of poverty. Education is regarded as a frill, as something which it may be quite nice to have, but which may have to be postponed due to other considerations, medical or social.

Such were the kinds of issues with which the inquiry was going to concern itself. And so, happily innocent, I met the civil servant who was to be in overall charge of the servicing of the committee, and the young principal, who was to be its secretary. The first of these was a curiously ineffective and plaintive man called Michael Walker, whose sister Micheline had been a school-friend of my older sister, Grizel, and had been much mocked and despised by us younger ones when she used to come to stay. So I suppose I expected little from Walker from the beginning. The secretary, John Hedger, however, was enthusiastic, energetic and intelligent. I took to him immediately, and knew I would enjoy working with him, as turned out to be the case, until he was moved on.

I was offered the chance to make suggestions about membership of the committee, but my ignorance prevented my contributing much. The only person I really wanted as a member was Lucy Faithful, then head of social services in Oxford. I did not know her well at that time (though later when we were both in the House of Lords she became a great and much-admired friend), but I knew that she was particularly concerned with the education of children in care, which

I believed to be an important issue. However, I was not allowed to have her as a member, being told simply that she was 'not *persona grata*' in the department. From the start, therefore, I realized that there were things going on in the background which I should probably never fully understand; and that I must take extreme care not to be used simply as a tool to implement an already fixed departmental agenda.

There were many reasons for setting up a committee of inquiry into special education in the early 1970s. It had long been acknowledged that provision was less than ideal, and was in any case patchy and uncoordinated. There was a general feeling that special education was something easily forgotten, and that children in receipt of it were pushed away, out of sight and out of mind. As long ago as 1944, when the Butler Education Act was introduced, an ideal was articulated which had never been fully realized. In the debate on the Education Act that year, the Parliamentary Secretary for Education, Mr Chuter Ede, speaking in the House of Commons, said:

> ... I do not want to insert in the Bill any words which make it appear that the way to deal with a child who suffers from any ... disability is to be put into a special school where he will be segregated. Whilst we desire to see adequate provision of special schools, we also desire to see as many children as possible retained in the normal stream of school life.

He estimated that special education was needed for up to 17 per cent of the school population, and that ordinary schools would have a major share in providing it. (This turned out to be very close to what we would say in 1978.) However, what he hoped for did not come about. Special education became a narrow concept, and provision in ordinary schools did not materialize, largely because, after the war, local education authorities (LEAs) had great difficulty in supplying places for 'normal' children in ordinary schools, and there was simply no money to close special schools, or join them to mainstream schools. Moreover, the allocation of children to different types of school was dominated by IQ testing until the 1960s, and this made segregation almost inevitable, at least for the mentally disabled. There was thus a sense of an unfinished agenda.

But the introduction of comprehensive schools in the 1960s and 1970s made the original vision of special educational provision in mainstream schools seem more possible. I was to discover how central to the thinking about special education was the question of where such education was to be provided; indeed there was a danger of this question coming to dominate the discussions of the committee, as well as to dictate the expectations of the educational press and public. All the press leaks before we actually reported announced that we were going to recommend that all handicapped children should be educated in mainstream schools.

Apart from these long-standing and general considerations, there were also more immediate reasons for setting up a committee. Doubtless because of a gradual change in attitude towards disability, legislation had been introduced in 1970, which came onto the statute book in April 1971, making all children, whatever their disabilities, the responsibility of LEAs, to be educated, not merely cared for. Hitherto, the most severely disabled children had been deemed ineducable, and were the responsibility of either the social or the health services, being either at home, or in hospitals, or in junior training centres or special care units.

33

In all, about 40,000 children had become entitled to education with the passage of the new legislation, and LEAs were greatly in need of guidance or regulation to enable them to take on their new duties.

One remarkable man constituted in himself a reason for taking action. This was Stan Segal, an enthusiastic and devoted teacher of the severely mentally disabled, an experienced lobbyist and a thorn in the flesh of government and the Department of Education. He wrote a book entitled *No Child is Ineducable*, and sent a copy to every MP and every member of the House of Lords. The book was extraordinarily persuasive, full of case-histories illustrating the difference education could make even to those hitherto regarded as hopelessly out of reach of its effects. It quickly sold out, and Robert Maxwell, then chairman of Pergamon Press, gave a huge party to launch the second edition, on 22 May 1974. I liked Stan Segal very much, and found his faith irresistible. Much as the civil servants laughed at his lack of professionalism, it was impossible not to be impressed by what he did, and what he demanded of others (including his own family) in running his residential school at Crowthorne in Berkshire. I suppose it was at this party, where I met such a gathering of knowledgeable and devoted experts, that I first began to realize the size of the task I had taken on.

Such considerations as these determined the Conservative government to set up the committee. People are prone to say that when governments cannot decide what to do, or want to postpone action and delay expenditure while seeming to take a problem seriously, they have recourse to a committee of inquiry, whose report they can then, in due course, receive and, if they so wish, reject or put on one side. There is no doubt a grain of truth in this. But I have not found governments neglectful, on the whole, of the output of committees of which I have been a member; in fact in the case of this particular committee I have been appalled to reflect how much of what we recommended was incorporated in the 1981 Education Act, even those parts that would have benefited from further scrutiny and alteration.

Of committees of inquiry in general it is also often said that they consist only of a certain kind of establishment person, always the same, with only a narrow range of experience; and that, being appointed, not elected, they have no authority to pontificate or to offer advice to ministers. They are, in the derisory phrase, 'the Great and the Good.' Again, there is truth in these charges. On the other hand, the essential criterion by which to judge if a committee is likely to be useful is whether its members will be able to give time to it, will not only read the papers but turn up to meetings. It is extremely difficult, for example, to have practising barristers as committee members, excellent though they often are, because they can never predict for how many days they may be obliged to appear in court on a particular case. There is nothing more time-consuming than having to go through arguments for a second time, because someone who has missed a meeting quite properly feels entitled to question and perhaps overturn what has been settled in their absence. One cannot altogether eliminate this hazard, but it leads to inefficiency.

Moreover, since membership of such committees is generally not paid, it is almost inevitable that the committees will consist mainly of people who are reasonably affluent, or who have retired from professional life and can to a certain extent dictate their own schedules of work. But, despite such drawbacks, the main and enormous advantage that such committees have over working groups of civil servants is that their membership is public knowledge; individual members as well as the committee as a whole can be lobbied and must be prepared to demonstrate that their conclusions have not been reached in haste or as a result of blind prejudice. Their final report comes not as anonymous advice, but as a document in the public domain. Though not elected, they are nevertheless accountable. (In this respect they are preferable to the 'focus groups' now in fashion. In the old days, at least, there was some real attempt to ensure that appointments to quangos were, if not apolitical, at least reasonably balanced.)

Having met both my Civil Service minder and the secretary of the committee, and having had them both, separately, to lunch in Oxford to try find out what they were going to be like in this strange relationship, colleagues and yet not colleagues, sometimes to be deferred to for their knowledge of the field, sometimes to be opposed or questioned, I then met the man who had been put on the committee specifically in the role of vice-chairman. He was a nice, solid, comfortable man called George Cooke who was County Education Officer for Lincolnshire, and was immediately reassuring. He was proud of Lincolnshire, and later, when we visited a teacher training college in Lincoln, he took members of the committee on a tour of Lincoln Cathedral, which included climbing up to the roof and seeing the massive beams of wood stored up there for future use, and looking down, terrifyingly, on the blue-cassocked choir singing evensong, as it seemed, miles below.

I had the feeling that George Cooke was in some way disappointed. Perhaps he had hoped to chair the committee, but I don't think so. I think rather that he saw the way education was going to develop, and did not much like it. In any case he was unendingly kind to me, and used to address me as 'dear'. I went to meet him for the first time in the

Department of Education in York Road, in a small and infinitely uncomfortable room; and I could not but be struck by the extreme difference from the meeting I had just left, which was of the IBA (of which I was a member for nine years, from 1972), where the surroundings, though not beautiful, were luxurious, and where members of the IBA were treated like royalty by the permanent staff and their secretaries. York Road, by contrast, was not smart.

The first full meeting of the committee took place on 17 September 1974. I was horrified by its size; there were 26 committee members and, it seemed, innumerable observers, advisers and hangers-on. Since our report was to cover Scotland as well as England and Wales (although not Northern Ireland), there had to be observers and advisers from Scotland as well. All through the writing of the report we had to be constantly alert to the differences between Scottish arrangements and those in the rest of Britain. 'But not in Scotland' became a perpetual refrain. A junior minister from the Department of Education attended part of this meeting and stayed to lunch. But I cannot even remember who he was; and I remember nothing of his welcoming speech, nor of my mumbled reply. I remember simply that I gazed round the assembled faces thinking that I would never learn the difference between one person and another, nor become accustomed to the hideous, low-ceilinged rooms of the department, and the unending noise of trains coming in and out of Waterloo station, far below.

These trains indeed haunted us for the next three and a half years. We used to meet on the top floor of York House, which became exceedingly hot in the summer. Yet if we opened the windows, though we could just about breathe, we could hear nothing except the genteel voice of the lady on the tannoy, announcing that the next train to depart from platform something was for Basingstoke, Micheldever, Winchester and Southampton. This for me, though a distraction, was curiously soothing, since I was brought up in a house not far from the station in Winchester, and when the wind was in the right direction, I could hear those same stations called out as I lay in bed in the night-nursery. It was perhaps this cosiness that so often induced in me a state of almost ineluctable slumber. This, however, was all in the future.

Our next meeting was more productive than the first. We at least managed to settle how we should proceed: there would be subgroups to deal with various topics, some of them related to specific handicaps, but mostly divided according to the age of the children or young people, or according to whether we were concerned with relations with parents, with LEAs or with professionals such as doctors or social workers. We had an important group concerned with the training of teachers, and another one with the curriculum (which was to cause us terrible problems). On the whole we did not have to change this structure much as we went along; and it meant that the piles of written evidence could be read by the appropriate subgroups, rather than by everyone. The groups mostly formed themselves naturally according to the expertise of the members, and every member was on at least two groups. The groups were not to be chaired by me, but by someone who was, more or less, expert in the field. On the whole people were content with this arrangement, though I could tell that there were some who felt that they would not have enough power over the final outcome. But I assured them, even on this first proper occasion, that the drafts from the subgroups would be subject to scrutiny by the full committee. I came away this time having more or less sorted out who everyone was, certain that there were going to be some people whom I would find a great nuisance, and others whom I thought I might get to like.

At this stage of the life of a committee I, at least, am enormously (though not always permanently) struck by the superficial appearance, clothes and general demeanour of the members. There was one person to whom I instantly felt attracted. I could tell that she was witty, a bit dogmatic, unafraid; that she was tall and well dressed, in clothes that looked vaguely 1920s – a somewhat Virginia Woolf look. As we came away we met on the underground station, and were both going to Paddington. Her first remark was 'Well! No lovers for us, I fear.' We then fell to, and talked without ceasing until we parted at Didcot. She was Winifred Tumim, wife of the lawyer Stephen Tumim, later to be Chief Inspector of Prisons. She had read PPE at Lady Margaret Hall, and we had had the same tutor. Both of her parents had recently been killed in an air crash, and she had inherited quite a lot of money, I think. She had two profoundly deaf daughters (and one hearing daughter), and was at that time embroiled in hideous controversies about the way deaf children should be taught. Later she went to America to study a new kind of sign-language, and she did a doctorate at London University, based on her own experience of teaching her daughters, and arguing that one could determine, when deaf children are quite young, whether they will be able to flourish in the hearing world, or will be happier in the deaf world; this difference could be shown by how easy or difficult it was to teach them abstract concepts. All this happened later; at the time, I was delighted to have found someone whom I could think of, and still think of, as a friend, a most unusual, distinguished and above all amusing person. What luck. Even so, writing about this meeting immediately after it, I commented that it was 'not a nice committee: too big, dowdy, and full of vested interests. I hate it, and probably always shall.'

There was one other person on the committee who gradually became, and remains, though not a lover, a great friend and support (and probably all the better for not being a lover). This was Philip Graham, a child psychiatrist, specialising in adolescence, who worked at the Great Ormond Street Hospital for Sick Children, and who became a professor during the lifetime of the committee. He was a tall bony man, Jewish, with black hair and blue eyes, with an analytic intelligence, powers of disconcertingly sharp observation, and a direct manner. He was often critical of what I did, but never bullying or unsympathetic. He was by far the cleverest member of the committee, and the most wide-ranging in his interests. We still meet quite often, and there is always an immense amount to talk about. He is a bit shocked by what he regards, probably, as my snobbishness (he must be the least snobbish man in the world; I remember being amazed, soon after I first knew him, when he told me that he and his wife were taking their children to a Pontin's camp for their holidays) and my politics, far less left-wing than his – last time we met, he said, sadly, 'I thought you were one of us', but he can't really have thought that.

At any rate, he never minded ticking me off. I had insisted that we must always have wine at our lunches in the middle of meetings (I would not be able to do that now). He thought I drank too much at lunch and then went to sleep, though he was admiring of how I managed to intervene, usually rather sharply, while apparently in this torpid condition. There was also a day when we were travelling somewhere on a visit and he came and sat by me in the carriage saying 'there is something I must say to you.' My heart sank. It reminded me of when my mother used to say 'I must speak to you.' (It is amazing what emotive force words like 'say' and 'speak' can have in certain contexts.) Anyway, what he had to say was indeed a reproach. He had noticed that I called all the members of the committee by their Christian names except one person, whom, he said, I manifestly disliked. I did, it is true, find her awkward, reopening a topic when I thought I had wrapped it up, with the words 'One last point ...' (How did she know it would be the last point?) Anyway, I said humbly that I didn't even know what her Christian name was; and he told me. I think I managed to use her Christian name once, but no more.

I suppose I got to know Philip properly when we spent ten days in America on committee business, early in 1977. Various groups of committee members visited different countries, Norway, Germany, Holland and the United States. I was allowed to choose where I would go, and chose America largely because I could combine visits to schools and hospitals with visits to friends. Otherwise I had no say in who went where. There were two other members of our group, John Fish, a schools' inspector, who was an indispensable adviser to the committee, and a Scottish educational psychologist, Peter Priestly, who appeared to me to be of a nervous disposition and something of a hypochondriac, though so pale, silent and sick-looking did he become as the days went by that I began to fear that he was really ill. (It is astonishing how one gets to know and apparently see into the nature of people on such intense and campaign-like working trips, a mixture of the cruise and the boarding school.) Peter Priestly did not care for getting up early, nor for sight-seeing, nor travelling into what he thought were dangerous and uncharted waters; John Fish, who liked all these things, was so kindly a man that he usually elected to stay with Priestly. This left Philip and me to pursue our own adventures. One morning we got up at 5.30, in the most extreme cold I have ever experienced, to take the ferry to Staten Island. The sky gradually became an intense blue, and the sea was partly frozen in great white lumps. Philip was in even greater agony of cold than I was, because he had lost one of his enormous Icelandic woollen gloves. Our faces were frozen, and we settled for a huge breakfast in a diner when we got there, eggs and pancakes and masses of coffee, the most marvellous meal imaginable.

Another day we went to a large hospital in Harlem to visit an American friend of Philip, Virginia Wilking, who ran the psychiatric department there. We saw a number of her day-units, which were run as day-schools for children with emotional and behavioural disorders of varying degrees of severity, and I was extraordinarily impressed by the humanity, optimism and efficiency of this tall, somewhat floundering woman, apparently isolated in Harlem, but utterly absorbed by her work.

We had come to the hospital in a taxi, but decided we could not afford a taxi back, and so walked a few blocks to the subway. I was terrified. The apartment blocks were crumbling, snow was piled up on the pavements, in spite of the freezing cold there were threatening groups of black men and boys standing at their doors staring at us as we went past, and sometimes moving to follow us, or calling out to the next group to stop us. I stared straight ahead, but once glanced at what I thought of as the reassuring figure of Philip stalking grimly along beside me. Surely we were safe, with him in charge. When we finally got into our train, I found that Philip was shaking and ashen, just as much frightened as I was; and when, later in the day, we told an American doctor what we had done, he said that we had taken an absolutely insane risk.

I was discovering that chairing a committee of inquiry was both like and unlike teaching, the professional activity I have most enjoyed in my life. It is like it in that, whether you are teaching one person alone, a small group or a class of 30, it is inevitable, and necessary, that you get involved with the personalities of your pupils: what their recurring characteristics are, what enlivens or depresses them, what seem to be the obstacles to carrying them with you. If you do not do this your teaching will be mechanical and probably ineffective. So it is that, in trying to tell what chairing a committee was actually like, I have first thought about the people who made up the committee, and who served it.

Secondly, it is like in that it has to be you as chairman or you as teacher who is responsible for the structure of the discussion. Every now and then you may feel confident enough to loosen the reins and let the class, or the committee, have its head, but always knowing that you, like a competent rider, can, when you so decide, collect the reins, reduce the pace and take charge again. (I suppose that my enormous pleasure in riding was, as my husband would have said, derived from a lust for power, just as my pleasure in schoolteaching was. But this would not particularly alarm me. As I have said, I believe that the desire for power is an extremely potent force in human psychology, as most political philosophers, from Plato, through Hobbes, to Nietzsche have recognized.)

On the other hand, the immense and overriding difference between a committee of inquiry and a class is that, at least in my case, every member of the committee knows more about the subject (even if not about every aspect of it) than the chairman. We were all engaged in the process of inquiry and recommendation together; but, on the way, it was I who was learning, they who were teaching. Both members of the committee and those whom we called to give evidence, as well as those consulted by the particular subgroups who were charged with producing separate draft chapters, were possessed of an immense body of knowledge and expertise, and from them I gradually acquired some sense of what special education was and what it could achieve.

As I have said, we were conducting our deliberations at a time when it had only recently been recognized that every child, whatever his or her disabilities, could benefit not just from care but from education. My understanding of this grew at the hands of my teachers. For example I learned from Professor Mittler of the Department of Special Education at Birmingham University (who gave generous help to the committee in all kinds of ways), how the parents of disabled children, brought together in groups along with their children, could be taught themselves to teach their children things which other children would learn spontaneously. I learned from him also how a child who was completely inert, could not move, did not understand what was meant by pointing at something, let alone naming it, could gradually and with infinite patience be taught step-by-step what pointing meant, how himself to point to indicate preference, and perhaps finally to move towards the things he wanted, even to vocalize, to indicate that he would prefer the radio to listen to rather than the teddy-bear to play with. I learned what others had probably understood all the time, that such progress as this could not come about without teaching; and that it was therefore *educational* progress. Moreover, I learned that the difference such education made to a severely handicapped child was immense. It was the difference between self-determination, or freedom, albeit extremely limited, and total dependency and indifference to the real world.

Part of my learning process was to go round numerous schools, special schools, or specialized units attached to mainstream schools, usually accompanied by John Hedger, though occasionally with other members of the committee as well. In this way I became directly familiar with children with disabilities such as I had never encountered before, and with their teachers. I began to enjoy enormously this part of the work, though it was sometimes depressing, and sometimes seemed actually alarming. I remember going to a special school in Liverpool, where I was approached and hugged by a black boy, about six foot tall and very strong, who asked, in urgent tones, 'Are you Liverpool or Everton?' I felt as if my life might literally depend on my answer, so I managed to breathe out that I was a supporter of Leeds United, and he let me go.

Going about with John Hedger was invariably enjoyable. He had small sons of his own, and was good at getting on with children, so we used to dawdle round the classrooms, talking to pupils and looking at their work. We always ran behind schedule. He had become genuinely fond of disabled and potentially helpless children. I remember one day when we were driving together to visit some school, we saw, nowhere near the school to which we were heading, a mother walking along with a child who was behaving very oddly, and John said lovingly, 'I think he must be one of ours.' I sometimes wondered whether it was because he was getting too greatly involved, for a civil servant, that he was moved on to another job. I deeply regretted his departure.

By the summer of 1976, about half way through the life of the committee, he was replaced by a very different character,

Imogen Luxton, who remained our secretary until the end, and with whom I therefore had to struggle in actually writing the report. Poor Imogen; we did not get on, and she disapproved of me profoundly. She also had problems about working long hours without a break – a regime I sometimes imposed on her. She had, every now and then, a bad back, which meant that I had to carry her luggage if we were travelling; and she could not sleep if there was noise. I recall an occasion when we stayed in a hotel in Glasgow, where a wedding was being celebrated with an all-night party, and her room was situated just above the racket (which was indeed horrendous). The management could not find her another room, so the only thing to do was for me to swap with her, an outcome which she seemed to accept as of right. She was well dressed and ladylike, and seemed to display no interest in the children with whom we were concerned. Luckily, by the time she arrived the routine of visits, the fact-finding, was more or less over, so I never had to go to schools with her. Soon after she joined us, Michael Walker retired, and was replaced by a more colourful figure called Vivien Stevens, of whom Imogen appeared to disapprove, and whom I came to like only slowly. But he very seldom turned up at meetings, so the change was hardly noticeable.

Shortly after Imogen had arrived, and just before Michael Walker left, we convened for a residential session on the outskirts of Cardiff, in the Llandaff College of Education. I have seldom before been to a place which actually made me weep, but this did. The rooms were tiny, the beds, two to a room, were agonizingly uncomfortable sofa-beds, the floors were bare, the bathrooms far distant. The food we were offered was appalling. Everyone was bad-tempered. We were supposed to be going through all the draft reports submitted by the different subgroups, but there was a revolution. The committee demanded that we should first consider the structure of the whole report, or, they said, they could not know what they were writing their separate bits for. It was time to stop working in the dark. I was convinced that they were right. Imogen was understandably furious, because she had drawn up an agenda which had not anticipated so radical a discussion. Michael Walker bleated pathetically that we none of us had the long experience that he had, which told him that it would be wrong to think about structure before we had heard all the evidence that was still to be heard. I sided strongly with the committee because, though I had enjoyed a year of learning about things quite new to me, I now longed to get some idea of what all this learning added up to. Why did we think special education needed to be rethought? What status did we think it should have? I believed that it was time to formulate some kind of collective vision, and to provide a framework within which all the details we were putting together could be organized and rendered persuasive.

To his great credit, though he had opposed the proposal to consider a structure for the report, Michael Walker worked very hard, more or less through the first night, outlining something he thought might do (assisted by Imogen). The next morning it was plain that there was going to be trouble. I had also worked through the night, writing a somewhat rhetorical introduction to the report, setting out what I had come to believe were our general aims for the education of handicapped children, as an aspect of education in general. However, one member of the committee, Sir Ted Britten, then recently retired General Secretary of the National Union of Teachers, had his own agenda. He came to the morning meeting with a short statement to the effect that, in a country devoted to the ideal of educating all children in the same schools, whatever their abilities, our aim must be the abolition of special schools and an end to educational segregation. Of my proposed introduction, he said it was philosophical, and therefore irrelevant. After all, everyone knew what the aims of education were. There was no need for us to state them.

So far, in the life of the committee, Ted Britten had been implacably hostile to me, openly declaring to other members and even to the press that it was a Tory plot that I, so manifestly elitist, as well as ignorant, should have been appointed chairman. He chaired the teacher training subgroup, of which I was, by choice, a member, and we had fairly frequent arguments about what might and what might not be expected of ordinary classroom teachers. He was almost equally hostile to Philip Graham, on the grounds that he was an advocate of boarding education for some disturbed children. This was absurd ground on which to fight the class war; as I have said, no one could be less snobbish than Philip, and none of his children attended a boarding school. But, in Britten's book, there was no such thing as a good boarding school of whatever kind. He constantly referred to me as 'a boarding school product', suggesting that this completely overthrew any credibility I might otherwise have had. All the same, in many ways I liked and respected him ('respect' as one respects a force of nature), not only because of his passionate consistency, his apparent determination to stick to his principles, but because of an element of realism, ultimately showing through the ideology. (It was he who argued that our report would be worthless to ministers unless we made a serious attempt to cost all our proposals. I had sympathy with this, but knew that we could not do so without imposing an immense burden on the department, which it was unwilling to undertake. Besides, in a time of inflation, costing was probably a waste of effort.)

Ted Britten's contribution, crucial at this meeting, was just about to lead to an argument, which would doubtless have become acrimonious, about whether our report should not try to avoid party politics, when Winifred Tumim most happily intervened. She said that we must have philosophy in the introduction, but we needed to go further back than I had gone. We needed to raise and answer the question of why severely handicapped children should be educated at all. After all, she argued, numbers of children now survive who would have died in infancy in earlier times. Now we have children who are referred to as 'vegetables' or as 'cabbages' ... 'a veritable market garden'. Why should money be spent on their education? This intervention saved the day (as well as having the desirable effect of making people laugh). We spent the rest of the morning debating what we should say about the point of educating the most severely disabled, as, after all, the law had demanded since 1971. We came up with the unoriginal, but truthful, dictum that education was something that everyone agreed was a good to which in a civilized country all were entitled; and that therefore justice and humanity demanded that no one should be automatically excluded from its benefits.

This led us naturally back to the task of defining education in terms of goals which should be aimed at for all children, whatever their abilities. Ted Britten suddenly became fired with enthusiasm for this way of thinking, and jumped up to a blackboard, on which he drew a line, representing the continuum of educational needs, with the very severe at one end, the minor or temporary at the other. This was an idea that had been put forward in the United States, by the

Council for Exceptional Children, in 1974.* For the time being the question of where children should be educated was forgotten, swallowed up in the questions why they should be, and what could bring their education about. Everyone was relieved, I think, that the threatened row between Ted and me had been at least postponed. We fell to enthusiastically, all sixteen of us (except that one of our number had passed out earlier in the meeting, been efficiently diagnosed by the psychiatrist and the paediatrician among us as suffering from a sudden drop in blood sugar, and had been removed). Even the observers and hangers-on joined in, including (which was rare) those from Scotland.

At last I managed to change Ted Britten's diagrammatic line to a more pictorial road, along which all children set out to tramp towards some distant goals. I, going back to my original rhetoric, named the goals provisionally as Knowledge, Experience, Imaginative Understanding and Pleasure. These goals got tinkered with and changed from time to time; there was especial hostility to the inclusion of pleasure as a goal. The civil servants, in particular, could not reconcile themselves to the thought that billions of pounds a year should be spent on the pursuit of pleasure.

But the use of the goals remained. The road towards them was seen as smooth and easy for some, fraught with obstacles and difficulties for others. Special education was a matter of helping children over the obstacles, one by one. It was giving them what they needed to make progress towards the common goals. So it was that that very day we had decided, if not on the detailed structure of the report, at least on the broad direction in which we were to go. And we

---

* See Elizabeth Anderson, *Journal of Child Psychology and Psychiatry*, 1976/77: 152.

decided there and then that our report should appear under the title 'special educational needs', with no reference to either 'handicap' or 'disability'. The vision of the common path served us well.

The outcome of our deliberations that day appeared in the final report as paragraph 1.4, and the following paragraphs. It is worth quoting, because the germs both of the success of the report, such as it was, and of the ultimate quagmire into which the concept of special educational needs has led us are to be found in it:

> 1.4 We hold that education has certain long-term goals, that it has a general point or purpose, which can be definitely, though generally, stated. The goals are twofold, different from each other, but by no means incompatible. They are, first, to enlarge a child's knowledge, experience and imaginative understanding, and thus his awareness of moral values and capacity for enjoyment; and secondly to enable him to enter the world after formal education is over, as an active participant in society and a responsible contributor to it, capable of achieving as much independence as possible. The educational needs of every child are determined in relation to these goals. We are fully aware that for some children the first of these goals can be approached only by minute, though for them highly significant, steps, while the second may never be achieved. But this does not entail that for these children the goals are different. The purpose of education for all children is the same; the goals are the same. But the help that individual children need in progressing towards them will be different. Whereas for some the road they have to travel towards the goals

is smooth and easy, for others it is fraught with obstacles. For some the obstacles are so daunting that, even with the greatest possible help, they will not get very far. Nevertheless, for them, too, progress will be possible, and their educational needs will be fulfilled, as they gradually overcome one obstacle after another on the way.

1.5 Broadly, our task has been to consider how teaching and learning can best be brought about wherever there are children who have particular obstacles to overcome, whether these are primarily physical, sensory, intellectual or emotional...

1.6 The criterion by which to judge the quality of educational provision is the extent to which it leads a pupil towards the twin goals which we have described, towards understanding, awareness of moral values and enjoyment and towards the possibility of independence. It is progress towards these goals which alone can justify a particular course of education for anyone, whatever his abilities or disabilities. For some children, enjoyment and understanding may be confined to the hard-won, taught capacity to recognize things and people and perhaps to name them. For some, indeed, independence may in the end amount to no more than the freedom to perform a task oneself rather than have someone else do it, even if the task is only getting dressed or feeding oneself. For others the concepts of imaginative understanding, enjoyment and freedom have infinitely richer content. But the direction of progress is the same.

The noticeable thing about these paragraphs is that they omit any reference to different categories or degrees of disability;

and they leave entirely open the question of where or alongside whom the children are to be helped to overcome those obstacles with reference to which their educational need is established. This was certainly what struck many of those who came to read the report when it was published. It was clear that we were concerned as much with children who might have a temporary or minor disability, such as conductive deafness, as with those who had permanent sensory deprivation or brain damage. In the case of all of them, the question was not so much what was wrong with them as how could they be helped to make progress.

I was once, soon after publication, asked to lunch in the Athenaeum by a senior civil servant, whom I knew but did not very much like, regarding him as arrogant and a bit of a cold fish. I was surprised and alarmed by the invitation, but accepted it, nevertheless. He gave me an exceptionally good lunch, and then said, very formally, 'I brought you here to express my gratitude for what you have done.' It turned out that he had a mentally disabled son, aged eleven or twelve, and that since the report had been published people's attitude towards him had radically changed, and that included the attitude of the child's contemporaries. They regarded him for the first time as not much different from themselves; they played with him in the street, and took an interest in what he was doing and what he said. He was no longer a pariah. I was pleased, and I changed my opinion of my host. Ted Britten's concept of the continuum, and mine of the common educational road had, to this extent, worked.

Going back, after our breakthrough in Cardiff, our problems were by no means over. For example, given our much wider concept of special needs, in the light of which many children with educational needs would already be in mainstream schools, it seemed clear that all teachers ought to learn something about how to pick up the signs of a special need in their ordinary classroom teaching. Therefore we argued that some aspects of what constituted a special need, and how it might initially be dealt with, should form part of the curriculum in the training of teachers.

Both the associations of teacher trainers and the teachers' unions were wholly opposed to any such idea. They clung fast to the old and absolute distinction between special education and normal education. You couldn't expect ordinary teachers, even as students, to tangle with what was a quite different specialist subject. If they were to have anything to do with children with special needs they would have to be paid extra. Even Ted Britten, loyal though he was to the unions, became exasperated with such arguments. As for me, my face creaked and ached with the effort to smile and look pleasant when involved in these apparently endless disputes. Some members of the committee congratulated me on my patience, after one especially long drawn-out and irritating meeting. Before I could acknowledge the compliment, Philip Graham, ever sharp to discern what I was really thinking, said 'her patience is the thinnest veneer I have ever seen'.

Then of course the question of 'integration' did not go away for long. Once I had established that we were not going to recommend the abolition of all special schools, but were indeed going to try to ensure an enhanced role for them, as centres of advice and resources for the use of mainstream schools, then I fairly willingly put up with long tedious lists of different kinds of integration, special units, special classes, temporary withdrawal classes for the disruptive, and so on, all of which had a place in their own chapter in the report, though I doubt if they were much attended to.

Again, having argued for abandoning categories of disability as a way of targeting children with special needs, we nevertheless had to find some alternative means of referring to the children who experienced different needs. This led to a great deal of fairly futile discussion. Categories, 'the blind', 'the deaf', 'the mildly educationally subnormal (ESN (M))' or 'the severely educationally subnormal (ESN(S))', and so on, were at least grammatically manageable. Too often the alternative designations were simply more cumbersome. I could never quite get used to having to talk about 'schools for children with emotional and behavioural difficulties' instead of schools for the 'maladjusted'; and, though I could understand the objections to categorizing children or adults as 'subnormal', designating them instead as 'having learning difficulties' begins to sound absurd when the person who has these difficulties may be a grown-up, even aged. I am sure there were parents of dyslexic children who took some time to realize that this was, and still is, a forbidden word, in the department. Such children have 'specific learning difficulties'. However, the discussions we had about such terminological issues were relatively unimportant.

More serious in its consequences was the decision we took, as far as I remember without many dissenting voices, that in spite of our desire to move away from the old concentration on disabilities, it was necessary to seek to ensure proper educational provision for the most severely disabled, those who had until recently been deemed ineducable, by allowing them to be provided with statements of their needs. The local education authority would then, we recommended, have a statutory obligation to meet the needs listed in the statement, for example speech therapy, physiotherapy, or whatever might be necessary to improve the progress of the severely disabled child. Statements were also designed to ensure that if the family of a child moved to another area, they would go to their new local authority, statement of needs in hand. The concept of 'statementing', as it came to be called, has been one of the most controversial, and I suspect disastrous, aspects of special education, ever since it was first included in the 1981 Act, which followed our report. (I shall return to this below.)

As the time for finalizing the report drew near, at the end of 1977 and the beginning of the following year, our meetings became more frequent, and tempers became shorter. The vested interests on which I had commented after our very first meeting came more to the fore. Members began to insist that their own professions be given proper priority. The inherent conflict of interest between the social services and education, never far below the surface, was impossible now to disregard. For instance there existed a class of residential homes for children who had been taken into care by the LEA, which provided its own education on the premises (rather than sending children out to neighbouring schools). The teachers in these establishments were not employed by the LEA, but by the social services of the area. They were thus not subject to inspection of any kind, and no one from the LEA had any right of entry to the classes, so it was impossible to tell what provision was made in them for children with special needs.

If we had had Lucy Faithful on the committee, as I had wished, we could have investigated this anomaly, since it was precisely this with which she was concerned in Oxford; and because the move would have come from a director of social services, not from the LEA, progress would have been made. As it was, the people on the committee who represented the social services were extraordinarily defensive, suspecting that the education people (including me) despised them, and did not take them seriously. It became increasingly difficult to get people to recognize that it was with education, not 'care' that we were concerned, and that, in any case, the best way to 'care' for children, especially those who were socially disadvantaged, or whose behaviour was preventing their learning, was to get them into a condition where they could learn and could begin to experience the benefits of education. There were too many voices heard saying 'What does it matter if he can't read? The crucial thing is that he should have improved self-esteem.' My argument was simply that in a society which takes literacy for granted, self-esteem cannot coexist with illiteracy. We took evidence from several young people who had been in care for most of their childhood, and who had not learned to read until they were adults. Their evidence entirely confirmed my view; and I am sure that if we had been able to take evidence from young prisoners we would have had still more confirmation. This was the aspect of our report that I felt most strongly about, but we were not able to deal with it properly.

The reason for this became clear only when we had nearly finished. In January 1978 (our deadline for handing in the report was March) Philip Graham said that we must radically rethink what were to count as special needs, so as to give more attention to social deprivation. Immediately the social services people were up in arms, saying that this would be to invade their territory. We should concentrate on how children presented themselves at school, and leave their families out of it. This was of course absurd; we had already accepted a whole chapter on the idea of 'parents as partners'. But, as Philip pointed out, there were numerous children whose parents, far from being partners in the educational process, were actually themselves the cause of their children's educational failure. I managed to rewrite parts of the introductory chapter to meet the point, though only partially. I contrasted our view of special needs with the old view prevalent in 1944 which defined special education as 'education by special methods appropriate to pupils suffering from disability of mind or body'. I wrote in a paragraph in the chapter concerned with categories of disability that 'our view of special education is much broader and more positive ... it encompasses the whole range and variety of additional help, wherever it is provided, and whether on a full or part-time basis by which children can be helped to overcome educational difficulties, however they are caused' (3.38).

Feeble though these additions doubtless were, I presented them to Imogen for inclusion, and she did not appear pleased. She seemed to me to resent my insistence, from a much earlier time, on writing the report myself; and in all the long hours we sat in York House, while I wrote and she fed me material that other members had submitted, I believe this resentment grew. The trouble was that some of the drafts submitted were of such appalling unintelligibility that I could not have signed a report that contained them. It was a time when the vocabulary deployed by professional educationalists was becoming more and more choked with jargon. There was one draft on the curriculum submitted by the group headed by one Professor Philip Williams, a professor of education from Wales, which I had simply to send back to be rewritten, so abstract, abstruse and jungle-like was its style. Even nice John Fish, a man of clear head and sensible ideas, as well as wide knowledge of the field, came to pieces when he had a pen in his hand. It was a curious case of a failure, not of thoughts, but of words in which understandably to clothe them. I had once or twice had pupils who were the same, and I could never cure them. Anyway, I could not trust Imogen to sort out this tangle and indeed it was my own job to do so; and I believed that if anyone was actually to read the report it must have a single recognizable style.

At any rate, when I was trying to satisfy the need for some reference to social deprivation, in however weak a way, Imogen was cross; and then, when I had finished, she said 'They don't want it.' 'Who don't?' I asked (knowing quite well); and she said 'The Department.' It then emerged that she had been warned that in no circumstances was it to be suggested in our report that social deprivation (nor having English as a second language) was the cause of, or in any way related to, educational failure. I understood then that this was for fear of our seeming to be racist. (Later, in the year following our report, another committee was set up to look into the low standards achieved by West Indians in London schools. The first chairman of that committee was hounded out by accusations of racism; the second chairman was Michael Swann, a pretty tough nut, but in the end his report was neglected.) Sure enough, in the 1981 bill, which followed from our report, it was laid down on the face of the bill that a special educational need could not be deemed to exist on the grounds of social deprivation or of English being a second language.

At our penultimate meeting rebellion came from an unexpected quarter. The paediatrician member, one Sam Forrester from Manchester, had been a fairly silent member of the committee until now, indeed he had not been a particularly good attender. I thought of him, unfairly, as Soapy Sam. I felt that he set himself up as a non-stuffy eccentric, a professional odd-ball, in a somewhat ingratiating manner; but it has to be said that I had not got to know him at all well over the three and a half years we had, on and off, been meeting. In what I thought was a wholly innocuous part of the report concerned with children under the age of two (who, we recommended, should be allowed to receive education, if they had been found to have a disability), I had written that LEAs must work with health visitors and social services and must ensure that doctors passed on to them all relevant information after the birth of a disabled child, or after an impairment was later discovered. Sam Forrester came storming into the room with the draft in his hand, a transformed man. He said 'This is a resignation matter.' When I could get him to calm down, it turned out that it was the word 'ensure' that had inflamed him. No one, no one at all, could presume to 'ensure' that any doctor would do anything, let alone pass on confidential information to people who were not members of the profession. 'The profession will not stand for that kind of language', he shouted. The rest of the committee sat about bemused. Philip Graham, the only other member of the profession present, said 'Well I don't mind it; and if doctors are inclined to withhold information that will be relevant to a child's education, I think they should be made to divulge it.' I said 'How about "seek to ensure"? Would that be better?' But no. Forrester stood up again and said he was resigning. I finally persuaded him that it would be absurd to resign at this stage of our committee's life; and that I was sure that, in a cool hour, he and I could work out a wording that would satisfy him ('and Professor Graham', I sanctimoniously added). And so, after at least an hour's hard work we did.

By now the vanities, pomposities and the general self-importance of the members (many of them) had drawn Imogen and me together. We joined in being incredulous that so many trivial points could be dredged up to delay the signing of the report. One member found that we had neglected to pay tribute to the splendid work done by auxiliary nurses (or some other body of people) in the context of hospital schools. The committee had become the common enemy whom we were determined to outwit, if necessary deceive, if only the report might be signed and handed over to Margaret Beckett, then parliamentary secretary at the Department of Education and Science, at the appointed time. The final row was not between me and Imogen, but between me and Vivien Stevens. I had thought the final ceremony should be a matter for the committee and the Minister only. I thought that so we might have a jolly party, and part on good terms. But he decreed that all the advisers, observers and hangers-on who had dogged our footsteps from the beginning should also attend, and I had to give in.

The day dawned, 20 March 1978, and we assembled in a vast room in Gunnersbury Park. Just as we were about to inscribe our names, before Margaret Beckett arrived, and when we had all taken what I supposed would be a cursory glance at the final draft, there was a loud cry, and one of the members, who as far as I could remember had never spoken before, said, in tones of desperation, 'But what about the remedial gymnasts?' I got her to give me chapter and verse, and I wrote 'and the remedial gymnasts' in the report, without having time to discover what they were supposed to do, or in what circumstances. I just had time to exchange a genuinely conspiratorial glance with Imogen (who had earlier confessed that she was engaged to be married), when the Minister arrived. We had a jolly party, in spite of the hangers-on, at least after Mrs Beckett had left. There was a lot of embracing as we broke up, and for me the best thing was being kissed on both cheeks by Ted Britten who said, 'We were on opposite sides of the fence, but we have come together through reason.' And we agreed that this was both true and immensely encouraging.

So how was it? As I write those words, I hear Geoffrey's voice; it was the question we asked each other when either had been engaged in some enterprise without the other, or when together we had given a party, and wanted to go over it, to find out whether it could be judged a success. I have tried to explain truthfully what it was like. But the question remains whether the committee did well or badly. Was our party a success?

Immediately after the publication of the report it seemed that it had been. Although some people misunderstood, believing that the central message was the integration of the 'handicapped' with the 'normal', it gradually came to be seen that what we had done was to widen the scope of 'special needs', and that most of the children who had such needs, permanently or temporarily, were already in ordinary classrooms in mainstream schools. Our demands that different services should work together, our emphasis on the role of parents, and our recognition that parents of children with special educational needs must be given clear guidance through the jungle of LEA provision with the help of an approachable named person – all these aspects of our recommendations were widely welcomed. Even 'statementing' seemed to offer reassurance to parents and teachers of the most severely disabled. Moreover, teachers in special schools felt that their work had at last been recognized, and their particular expertise acknowledged. They had been brought in from isolation. From the teaching profession as a whole we got a warm welcome.

In 1976, when we were halfway through our deliberations, there seemed to be a danger that a bill would be introduced in parliament to give all parents the right to have their children educated in mainstream schools. I went to see Shirley Williams, Secretary of State for Education at the time, and had a long and extremely useful talk with her. As always, she was generous with her time, and quick and imaginative in her understanding of the issues. I begged her to try to defer legislation until our report had appeared. For one reason or another, the bill never materialized. And then, when the Conservatives came back in 1979, the new government was anxious to press ahead, and a bill based closely on our report was drafted, and became law in 1981. This seemed like success. However there was a monster fly in the ointment: no extra money was to be made available to LEAs for implementing the new procedures. And 1981 was in fact the beginning of the new era of educational cuts.

At the time I was most acutely aware of the impact of the cuts on the universities (Geoffrey became Vice-Chancellor of Oxford this year, and was deeply occupied with academic finances); but I began to realize almost immediately that our recommendations would not work unless LEAs could be allowed funds earmarked for special education. In particular there was a contradiction between their being obliged by the new law to provide everything that was needed for a child with a statement, and their having no new money. To make the mandatory provision for the most severely disabled, they would have to take money from elsewhere in their budget.

Within the next few years, I came to think, and I still think, that the invention of the statement was the greatest single mistake that we made. Parents had begun to believe that the only way they could get resources directed towards the special needs of their child was to press for him to be 'statemented'; LEAs varied widely in their response to this pressure. But because if a child was issued with a statement the LEA had a mandatory duty to supply what he had been found to need, the actual content of the statements became less like a true judgement of what would allow a child to make progress, and more like an estimate of what the LEA thought it would be able to afford. The appeals tribunal business was increasing all the time. Parents might appeal either on the grounds that their child had not been issued with a statement, or on the grounds that his needs, as defined in his statement, had not been met. But teachers were often reluctant to give evidence at the tribunals, the case against the LEA most often being answered by officers of that authority. The expenses of such tribunals were becoming enormous, the benefit to the child minimal. The climate of litigation, setting parents in conflict with LEAs, was far from conducive to imaginative thinking about how to improve the education of those children who for one reason or another had learning difficulties at school.

In 1993, in the foreword to a book of essays entitled *Special Education in Britain after Warnock,** I wrote:

> The point of the distinction between children with statements and those who, though identified as having special needs, had no statement was to ensure as far as possible that children with special needs were no longer regarded as a race apart. The aim was to demonstrate that there were large numbers of children, about 18 per cent of the whole school population who were in ordinary mainstream schools but who had special needs, There was a continuum of needs. This lesson has perhaps been learned. We are not so prone as we were in the early 1970s to think of 'the handicapped' as a particular weird class of persons. The other purpose of the statement was to ensure that

---

* John Visser and Graham Upton (eds), *Special Education in Britain after Warnock* (London: David Fulton, 1993).

those who had the most extreme and complicated disabilities would get the educational provision they needed, in whatever part of the country they lived, and that this right should be protected by law. But the distinction between those with and without statements, as the first Audit commission report of 1992 pointed out, was always vague and very difficult to incorporate in the law. Now that the system of statements is being widely abused, both by parental demand and by LEA failure to allow the needs of the child to dictate what goes into a statement, it seems to me time to get rid of what may be an obstacle to good and imaginative education for children in need. Such a change would not indicate a change of educational philosophy: it certainly would not indicate any lessening of the importance accorded to education in improving a child's life-chances. Far from it. It might be the next step forward in the battle to provide genuine access to education for every single child.

I would not change these words today. Later in 1993, in yet another Conservative Education Act, one section was devoted to an elaborate code of practice, to mark the various stages by which a child's special needs should be identified and met up to the point at which he might be issued with a statement. This went some way towards answering the criticism of the Audit Commission that the distinction between those with and those without statements were vague. But it did not meet the more general objections to the abuse of 'statementing'.

There are other reasons for pessimism about special educational needs. The odds stacked against children with such needs had been increased by the so-called Great Educational

Reform Act of 1988, Kenneth Baker's creation, which saw the introduction of numerous forms of testing for children at school, and of the league tables, publication of which would bring in an element of competition between schools, and would lead standards, it was argued, to rise. The spirit of the free market had entered education, and since the criterion of what made a school a good school was its success in examinations, low-achieving children were an increasing burden on any school. At one stage in the 1980s and early 1990s, parents were supposed to have free access to any school (the idea of choice being the central pivot of Thatcherite conservatism), and it was supposed that low-achieving schools would simply wither away. No one gave much thought to what was supposed to become of the low-achieving children in such schools while the withering process went on. The 1981 Act began to seem astonishingly old-fashioned, the last gasp of welfarism in a world of hard-nosed competition.

One enormous weakness in our 1978 report was beginning to become clear; and it was one of which some of the committee had been aware at the time. This was a weakness in the concept of special educational needs with which we were working. In the collection of essays to which I have already referred,* Peter Mittler wrote:

> ... the majority of children with special educational needs in ordinary schools and in some of our special schools come predominantly from the poorest sections of society. Indeed it can be said that the problem of special needs is to a large extent a problem of poverty and social disadvantage. The fact that this is not

---

* Visser and Upton, *Special Education in Britain after Warnock*, p. 22.

generally recognized reflects the high profile of children
with physical sensory and cognitive disabilities who tend
to come from all sections of society, and whose parents
organize powerful lobbies to protect the interests of their
children. Unfortunately, parents of children with
moderate learning difficulties and emotional and
behavioural difficulties, as well as parents of low-
achieving children in ordinary schools, do not tend to
join local or national associations, with the result that
their views are not so forcefully represented.

We knew in the early 1970s that children with moderate
learning difficulties and with emotional and behavioural
disturbances formed by far the greatest number of children
with special educational needs. But to identify these children
with the socially deprived was, as Imogen had warned me,
more or less taboo. In relying on our central concept of
special needs, we had tried to get away from the negative or
'medical' model of special education being designed for
children with something wrong with them. We had not been
radical enough. We were still stuck with the idea that SEN
children (as they had come to be called) could be identified by
their individual impairments.

In saying this, I am not suggesting, as some radical
sociologists have, that there is really no such thing as a
special educational need, and that it is our hierarchical and
conformist society which has constructed such a concept,
perceiving children to have needs which, without such a
perception, would not exist. It seems to me important to
distinguish the false belief that society has created the concept of special needs from the true belief that many children's special needs arise out of poor social conditions, out
of homelessness, ignorance, violence and abuse in their

backgrounds. Such children have educational needs which it is the duty of society to meet, and which to a large extent we are failing to meet in schools, and, after that, disastrously failing to meet in young people's prisons.

We are much more keenly aware than we were in the 1970s of the huge gaps in achievement between the affluent and the 'underclass'. We have not yet found a way of diminishing this gap through education. It may be that our 1978 report went as far as it could in publicizing the problems of children with special educational needs, and demonstrating how many of them there were for whom no proper provision was being made. But in my view it is now high time to re-examine the whole SEN structure as set up in the 1981 Act. At present nearly a third of the entire education budget is spent on children who are identified as having special educational needs. Perhaps we should go back to a 'medical model', make as good provision as possible for children with identifiable impairment, and meanwhile direct attention, and resources, to education, social as well as academic, for those children most in need. An increase in the funding of nursery schools is a step in the right direction.

So, though it may have made a modest difference to educational thinking at the time, I would not judge our long drawn-out party to have had a successful outcome; and I believe that I at least, having no particular interests to cloud my vision, should have been more imaginative, clearer-headed, and have shown more political nous. Perhaps if Ted Britten had been able to press his demand that we should try to cost all our recommendations, the report would have been given a decent burial. As it is, its publication seems to me to have made people feel good; but the educational consequences, taking the school population as a whole, have been nugatory.

# 2 Human Fertilization and Embryology

There can hardly be a question of greater interest, whether to philosophers or to those who would not so describe themselves, than the question, What constitutes a human being? How and when does a new human individual come to exist? To what stage of development can one trace back the 'I' who is unique? Each one of us is a separate organism, conscious of our individuality; we can scarcely fail to be interested in the origin and value of that individuality.

Long before the discovery of genes or the mapping of the human genome, we had been accustomed to thinking of ourselves as the outcome of sexual intercourse between our parents, the fertilizing of egg by sperm, and, often, as a *pignus amoris*, a token or proof of love. Now, since 1978, when the world's first test-tube baby had been born in Greater Manchester, we had learned that human eggs could be fertilized by sperm in the laboratory, and an embryo created by the intervention of scientists, to be placed in a uterus and carried to term in a normal pregnancy. Would the resulting child feel differently about herself when she learned that her existence depended on new technology? Should such 'unnatural' methods be encouraged for the sake of alleviating infertility? Or was there something intrinsically wrong about a birth that could be separated from sexual intercourse? These were among the questions raised by the first birth by *in vitro* fertilization (IVF).

Leading on from them there arose further and less easily answered questions. Most people quite soon came to believe that there was nothing morally objectionable about IVF itself; but if such an 'artificial' birth were to be more than a lucky fluke, the techniques which made it possible must be better researched. There must be investigation of the methods of causing the egg to fertilize, and the safeguards needed to ensure that the embryo in the laboratory was provided with an environment that would enable it to develop normally. The process of fertilization itself and the development of the very early embryo were not well understood. For such research to take place, embryos must be developed in various experimental environments, and must be monitored, and then destroyed. It would be manifestly wrong to place in a woman's uterus an embryo that had been the subject of research. That would constitute a harm both to the woman and to the possible child.

So the question had to be raised whether it was morally tolerable either to fertilize eggs donated specifically for research, and then destroy the embryo that resulted, or to use embryos produced in the course of IVF treatment, but which were not needed for implantation. For drugs were given to women undergoing IVF treatment which caused them to produce an abnormally large number of eggs, so that there would be a better chance of there being some viable embryos available to start a pregnancy. There were thus often several 'spare' embryos which might be used for research. But was this to be deemed permissible?

No one would countenance the use of a child for research, still less its subsequent destruction. Was the embryo in the laboratory sufficiently different from a child to justify its use in research? Children, even if not yet legal persons, are generally thought of as potential or future persons; in any case each child is manifestly a human organism, individual and unique, and thus of intrinsic moral value, and worthy of protection. How far back in the developmental story of the child from the fertilization of its mother's egg ought the moral imperative of such esteem and protection to be traced? The genetic make-up of the future person is settled with the mixing of sperm with egg. Does this entail that in some sense that future person has also sprung into existence?

Aristotle had addressed such questions, basing his speculations about mammalian embryonic development on what observations he could make, and on intelligent guesswork. Of course he had no microscopes; and he was unaware of the existence of female eggs. He had held that there are three forms of life or 'soul' ($\psi\upsilon\chi\eta$). The first of these was the vegetative or nutritive, which informs all living things, plants as well as animals. This comes into existence immediately on fertilization, in the case of humans by the breathing force of the sperm ($\pi\nu\epsilon\upsilon\mu\alpha$) acting on the female blood in conception. Then immediately in the case of all animals the second form of life or soul came into existence: the 'sensitive' life. And finally, in human animals, the rational soul was mysteriously added, at 40 days from conception in male embryos, and at 90 days in females.

These speculations were rediscovered by Thomas Aquinas in the thirteenth century, and gradually became with few alterations the official doctrine of the Church, until at least the seventeenth century. Even now, the doctrine of Ensoulment is taken by the Roman Catholic Church from Aquinas, though it is conceded that no one can know exactly when it takes place. And so, to be on the safe side, it must be assumed that from 'the moment of conception' every embryo

71

is endowed with an immortal soul and must not be deliberately destroyed. Thus the moral status to be accorded to the very early embryo seemed to many people to raise fundamental questions about the nature and value of human life.

How are such moral questions to be settled? This was bound to become an issue in its own right, with the setting up of a committee of inquiry in 1982. Why should such a committee be listened to? With what authority could it speak? As a society, we are not prone to believe in 'moral experts', whose pronouncements would automatically command respect. Yet the committee was set up to advise ministers on possible legislation; and laws, in a matter such as this, where moral feelings are deeply engaged, must themselves be based on some roughly agreed morality, or they will not reach the statute book. The problem of moral diversity was raised by the very setting up of a committee of inquiry. And because of the novelty and intrinsic interest of the subject-matter, morally opposing views were made evident in every newspaper story and television documentary that covered it. Thus, from the outset, when the inquiry was set up, it was clear that the issues it was concerned with would attract a high degree of publicity, and that the feelings of the public would be greatly involved. For members of the committee, right from the start, there was enormous pressure from the media, and this did not always make it easy to discuss matters calmly, as is the duty of such committees.

Since the publication of the report, and the consequential legislation in 1990, scientific advances in the field of embryology, and especially knowledge of the human genome, and the parallel development of genetic manipulation, have advanced at a great rate. I shall deal with changes since 1990 in the following chapter. In this chapter I shall go back to what it was like when the committee was meeting, between

1982 and 1984, and try as far as possible to tell it as it seemed then, avoiding hindsight.

The year 1982 was an extremely busy one for me. I had a more than usually heavy teaching load in the various Oxford colleges to which I was attached; I was chairing a Home Office committee on the use of animals in the laboratory (see Chapter 4); and the passage of the 1981 Education Act on children and young people with special educational needs (see Chapter 1) had led to numbers of lecture engagements at home and abroad. Moreover, Geoffrey had become Vice-Chancellor of Oxford in the Michaelmas term of 1981, and there was the enjoyable but new tasks of entertaining and official business as Vice-Chancellor's wife. I felt I was just about (but no more) keeping my head above water.

In June of that year, I was rung up by the Department of Health and Social Security (DHSS) to ask if I would consider chairing a committee that was about to be set up to examine the issues surrounding new fertility treatments, including IVF. In 1978 the work of Dr Edwards and Mr Steptoe, among others, had led to the first successful birth by IVF, the fertilizing in the laboratory of a woman's egg with her husband's sperm, resulting in a 'test-tube baby'. For the first time in my life, I was hesitant. My first reaction was that, surely, they could think of someone else. Secondly, I was not sure that either Geoffrey or I would welcome the publicity that would inevitably follow such an appointment.

However, in talking it over with him, he and I became more and more interested in the moral and philosophical issues (to which I have already referred), that we could foresee arising in this novel context; in particular, the Department had said that the purpose of the committee would be to advise ministers on possible legislation to regulate, or even possibly to prohibit, future advances in the field; and we were both very much interested in the theoretical relation between morality and the law. So in the end I was persuaded, by the intrinsic interest of the subject matter, to say that I would allow my name to go forward. Later in June I got a letter from Norman Fowler, then Minister of Health, inviting me to take on the job, and I accepted. I recognized that this was the beginning of a new way of life, and a new subject about which I would urgently have to learn, from a base of total ignorance.

It was understandable that the government should have wished to set up a committee of inquiry. The birth of the first test-tube baby in 1978 had been greeted at first by excitement. But there had been an unfortunate television programme in 1978 when Mr Steptoe, the surgeon (an enormously humane man, and a very good pianist), had looked with genuine wonder and delight at the hours-old baby girl who had been born by the new technique, and had said 'we have created a life.' This was the beginning of the reaction. Here were scientists 'playing God'. Who were they to create life? The Roman Catholic Church was especially hostile to the possibility that had opened up of birth through any other than the 'natural' way, separating conception from sexual intercourse (and especially as IVF inevitably demanded masturbation by the father to provide sperm, which was in itself a sin). Public opinion swung against the new technique. The *Daily Mail*, which had offered a large sum of money to extend the hospital which Steptoe and Edwards had set up at Bourn Hall, outside Cambridge, withdrew the money after the foundations had been laid. There were strong demands that the use of the technique should be outlawed, and all further research prohibited by law. The general public, though they had learned about test-tube babies, were profoundly ignorant about the details of the technique, or the possible wider future uses of it. It was reasonable to set up a committee composed of scientists, lawyers, and lay people with various professional interests, to consider the issues (and other related issues) as far as possible without bias, and to diminish the likelihood that government would be accused either of being in the hands of ambitious scientists or of giving in to popular, media-led emotion.

In early July 1982 I interrupted a lovely solitary and peaceful holiday in the house Geoffrey and I had bought in Wiltshire the previous year (he as Vice-Chancellor had to stay in Oxford until August, except at weekends), to go up for the first time to the DHSS in their headquarters at Elephant and Castle. I met the two senior civil servants (whom I never met again) responsible for setting up the committee, and the young married woman who was to be one of its secretaries. We talked about the membership of the committee. I had nothing to contribute, except about the broad categories of people we should try to include, and had anyway learned my lesson about suggesting names. But I was told that they proposed to have a particular man on the committee who would combine the roles of being the Roman Catholic member and that of psychiatrist. It so happened that this man had come to Hertford College to preach in the college chapel one Sunday in the previous term. He had preached a sermon about the joys of sex which, both by its content and his manner of delivery, had caused Geoffrey and me acute embarrassment. So when I heard that he was proposed as a member of the committee I said I felt I could not really get on with him. I was told that there was no one else in the world who could fulfil the joint role that was to be allotted to him;

so I suggested that we have two people, a psychiatrist (if it was thought we must have one) and someone else to be the Roman Catholic member (which of course I recognized that we needed). So we left it like that.

Days went by, and at last Mr Nodder, one of the civil servants I had met, rang up to say that nobody else had been found, neither one person nor two, and the membership of the committee was to be announced within the next week. I thought I was defeated. But I wanted my views to be clear; so I said that I would be grateful if he would tell the Minister that I thought it a very bad way to start a committee if there was a member with whom the chairman knows that she could not work. When Mr Nodder, alarmed by my vehemence, asked why I objected to this person, I rudely replied that he gave me the creeps. And I told him he could tell the Minister that too, if he liked. The next day Norman Fowler rang up to say that two people had been found, a Professor of Psychological Medicine from Cardiff (with whom I had actually served on a committee before, and who was very good and amiable), and a Roman Catholic who was Professor of Clinical Neurology at the Institute of Neurology in London (and who turned out to be both extremely nice and a marvellous committee member). I told this story later to Frank Longford, who was an old friend, and who used to try to convert me to Roman Catholicism, until I persuaded him that being married to an Ulsterman with the deeply Protestant name of Warnock, I would undoubtedly be divorced if he succeeded. Frank understood what I was saying, but was deeply shocked by my frivolity, and thought I should not have dug my heels in over so irrational a prejudice.

The committee was to have two secretaries. One was a doctor in the Department, Jeremy Metters, who was extremely well-informed about all forms of infertility treatment, who understood the science involved, and who was in a position to find out, if he did not already know, what research was going on both in the UK and elsewhere in the world. We could not have written our report, and certainly not within the two years allotted to us, without him. He was also an imperturbable, good-tempered and supportive person. He went on later to work for the European Commission.

The other secretary was Jenny Croft. She was a graduate of Somerville who had read English. When I first met her she was about seven months pregnant and, understandably, looked enormous. But later she still did, and for some reason which I never understood she generally dressed as a Watteau milkmaid, with huge skirts, beneath which emerged a frilly petticoat, and little pointed-toe slippers. I do not know where she could find such clothes, except in some shop that specialized in fancy-dress, perhaps in Wardour Street. I once saw her dressed otherwise, when I gave lunch in Oxford to her and Jeremy Metters and the DHSS legal adviser, one day in 1983. Then she was wearing a scarlet dirndle skirt, an electric-blue satin blouse, strained to bursting over her bosom, and a little scarlet hat perched sideways on her head. The problem with her bizarre appearance was that it was hard to disregard it; it was a distraction which took one's mind off the job. And, besides, she was noisy. She had a somewhat grating voice in which she talked unstoppably, often interrupting what someone else was saying. Even Jeremy Metters was sometimes reduced to using that unmistakably angry phrase, 'Let me finish.' When not talking, she had a habit of clicking her biro in and out, which came near to driving me mad, as the tensions of the committee meetings built up towards the end of our corporate life. I often reflected that I would have found it difficult to stop her doing this if she had been my pupil; as it was, our particular relationship made it impossible for me to tell her to shut up, even if there had been a polite way of uttering such a command.

The membership of the committee was announced in the press on 24 July 1982. Immediately there was a flood of calls from the press, radio and television. There was at this stage nothing I could say to them. They already knew the terms of reference, which were 'To consider recent and potential developments in medicine and science related to human fertilization and embryology; to consider what policies and safeguards should be applied, including consideration of the social, ethical and legal implications of these developments; and to make recommendations.' The broad scope of the subject was therefore known. But throughout the life of the committee we had difficulty in deciding how much or how little publicity we wanted. The DHSS wanted as little as possible; on the other hand we needed to collect the opinions not just of experts but of the general public, and therefore it was right that there should be discussion of the issues in the media, and the better informed the discussions, the more useful would be the response to our request for evidence.

I may have gone too far in discussing the questions themselves, both in the popular media and in specialist philosophical journals. Yet I am not convinced that this did any harm, as long as the discussion was couched in general terms. However, at a late stage in our deliberations, when we were struggling to prepare a final draft of the report, and there were disagreements, inevitably, among members of the committee we suffered from one member, a distinguished elderly gynaecologist, Dame Josephine Barnes, who appeared to think it her right to pass on the details of our discussions to a contact she had on *The Times*. For some time I could not pin down the source of these leaks, which were tiresome, in so far as I and I think almost all my colleagues wanted to present our recommendations along with the arguments to support them, and reasoned notes of dissent, rather than to have to deal with speculation and rumour. When finally I was almost, though not entirely certain who was leaking, I had to pull myself together and say something (without any accusation) about how hard it was on the secretariat that this should happen, since they naturally fell under suspicion. Thereafter the leaks stopped; but by then we were almost ready to publish.

We were sometimes urged to hold some of our meetings in public, especially when we were taking oral evidence. These days, when there is a greater demand for 'transparency', we might have been obliged to do so. But I personally am not convinced of the benefits of open meetings; committees change their minds as they make progress in understanding, and it is not particularly desirable for the general public to listen in to the learning process, when individual members may say things they would later regret or wish to disavow.

The committee met for the first time on 14 October. Elephant and Castle is not the most charming part of London. In the old days of the special needs Committee (which now seemed part of a very distant past) I had thought the surroundings of Waterloo, and the old Department of Education in York House unappealing enough; but they were nothing to the DHSS, in its various conjoined buildings, Hannibal House, Alexander House and others. I generally drove to meetings, and was allowed a parking space. But those coming by Underground had to brave an extraordinarily smelly and threatening underpass to reach the buildings. Once inside, the most notable feature of the room

79

where we met was that it had no windows. It was placed somehow in the middle of a series of corridors, put down like a large steel box, lit by neon lights, and with luck, provided with some sort of air-conditioning. When this broke down, there was no air at all. I have never been prone to suffer from headaches, but here I did, as did all the other committee members and civil servants. The clicking of Jenny's pen became a torment. However, on this first day, I was full of admiration for Jenny's courage, and full of sympathy for her, because her baby daughter, her first child, had been desperately ill with asthma and pneumonia, and had come out of an incubator only the day before, and was still in intensive care. (I had been warned indeed that she probably would not be there.) In any case, understandably, today she was subdued.

The first meeting was a great deal better than the first meeting of the special needs committee. For one thing, it was a smaller committee (sixteen as opposed to twenty six); for another thing, Jeremy Metters had sent us very clear background papers during September, which everyone had read. Because of the smaller numbers, I found it far easier to distinguish one person from another, and meeting Ken Rawnsley, the Professor of Psychology, again made me feel that I had at least one ally. As usual, I formed instant judgements of at least some of the members. I had met Josephine Barnes before, and knew she could cause trouble; but luckily she professed admiration for me, and thought it an important bond that she had been a pupil years before at the Oxford High School, where I had much later been headmistress, and also that she was a graduate, as I was, of Lady Margaret Hall. I had also already met Jean Walker, the wife of the Bishop of Ely, a psychiatric social worker, whose husband had been a canon of Christ Church before he went to Ely.

She was the only person who did not speak on this first day, but sat looking thin and uneasy. I commented afterwards in my diary that we had actually made some progress in deciding how to proceed; and that this was entirely on account of the clarity of Jeremy Metters's papers in which he set out clearly the most important issues we would have to consider. During a horrible buffet lunch on this first day, in another windowless room, we were visited by the then Chief Medical Officer, Sir Henry Yellowlees, and Norman Fowler, the Minister. He seemed not to be at all interested in meeting the members of the committee, indeed I could not persuade him to do so. I rather patronizingly described him afterwards as 'amiable, cocky and a bit brash', but added that I liked him and got on with him, something which continued to be true.

All the way through the deliberations of this committee, I was acutely conscious of how little time we had; we had undertaken to report in June or July 1984, two years from when the committee was first announced. I was determined to meet this deadline, both because I did not want to go on working at the subject for more than two years, and also because I thought that ministers would be much more likely to pay heed to whatever we recommended if we produced our report when they wanted it. And there was such public anxiety about the whole topic that there was a danger that our recommendations would be overtaken by some perhaps hasty, perhaps unduly restrictive legislation, unless we could make ourselves punctual. I realized, of course, how much there was to learn in this time, quite apart from the drafting of a report.

My learning, and I believe that of all of the committee, even the medical members, was taken in hand by one indispensable member, Dr Anne McLaren. At our second meeting, in December 1982, she gave us a lecture, at my request, on the process of fertilization, how egg and sperm unite to become a single cell within the nucleus of which is contained the chromosomes, or collections of genes derived from both parents. She explained how, in a normal pregnancy, while the fertilized egg is still in the woman's upper fallopian tube it begins the process of division, known as cleavage, into two, then four, then sixteen cells; and how at the two- and four-cell stage the cells are totipotent, that is they have the capacity to develop into any kind of human tissue, or into the placenta. After the sixteen-cell stage has been reached, a space develops within the cluster of cells that is filled with fluid, and when the fluid has accumulated the cells together are known as a blastocyst. Then within the blastocyst, a thicker section becomes identifiable as the inner-cell mass. This is what will develop into an embryo proper, then a fetus and then, if all goes well, a baby. This was the development that had been achieved outside the body, in the test-tube, and at last an embryo so made had been successfully placed in a woman's uterus, had implanted itself there within the uterine wall, and had developed into the first test-tube baby.

It is astonishing to me now to realize how totally ignorant of this complex developmental story I and most of my colleagues were. Anne never despised our ignorance. She explained patiently, with clear diagrams, going back over the ground as often as we wanted. There were many other occasions later when I asked her to give us a lecture; this was only the first, and therefore, I suppose, the most striking. I remember thinking that I would like above all things to learn more, and especially to be Anne's pupil. She was a brilliant teacher. The concept of the early embryo as a loosely conjoined cluster of four totipotent cells became central to our thinking, as time went on; and for most of us, it was new. After all, the campaign Save the Unborn Child, at that time set up with the keen support of Mr Enoch Powell as a lobby to get parliament to prohibit the use of embryos in infertility research, took as its logo a picture of a curled-up fetus. Most people thought of the early embryo as a tiny homunculus, recognizably human. We were now learning to think of the gradual development of the embryo in a completely different way.

Anne Mclaren managed to teach us a great deal even in this first morning; and then after lunch we took the first oral evidence, from members of the Medical Research Council (MRC), of which Anne herself was at that time a member, as head of the Mammalian Development Unit. The MRC team was led by an old Oxford friend called Geoffrey Dawes. At the time he was Director of the Nuffield Institute for Medical Research in Oxford, and had published a highly influential book on fetal and neonatal physiology. He, though a scientist, was one of a group of friends who came to be known as the Dancing Economists in the 1950s and 1960s. In fact, though there were certainly economists among them, there were philosophers, political theorists and other academics as well, and they used often to give informal dances. At one such dance Geoffrey, my husband, became entranced by Margaret Dawes, this Geoffrey's wife, and danced with her all the evening. I was about eight months pregnant, and this Geoffrey kindly took me under his wing. We danced together, an incongruous pair, many times, while he explained to me about the work he was doing on pregnant sheep, and the development of sheep embryos, the precursors, perhaps, of Dolly. I did not take much of it in at the time, but I was reminded of it now. (The next day, Margaret Dawes had invited us round for pre-lunch drinks, it being a Sunday. As we walked home to lunch, my Geoffrey asked whether I had heard the sound of scales clattering from his eyes. In fact

Margaret Dawes was extremely nice, and eventually I used to see quite a lot of her.)

To return to Anne Maclaren. As time went on, I began to have great difficulty in thinking how to structure our report. The committee had been set up to consider questions that arose from infertility. Yet it soon became plain that there were problems related to the possible regulation of such procedures as AID (Artificial Insemination by Donor) which were not, or not necessarily, related to infertility. For example lesbian couples might wish to make use of AID, taking sperm, perhaps, from male homosexuals who had sympathy with them, and in such cases the question of infertility did not arise. Again, there were Muslim women who sought AID without the knowledge of their husbands, because it was assumed in their community that failure to conceive was always the result of female infertility. If they did not conceive, they were liable to be thrown out of the marital home without support. (This we learned from Mr Anisuddin, one of our members who was the legal president of the UK Immigrants' Advisory Service, a useful and helpful member, but one of whom we saw little, because we understood he was helping his clients in court.) Questions concerning surrogate mothers, equally, might arise when homosexual men wanted to bring up children who were at least half genetically their own.

All these issues raised problems of possible regulation, of the proper screening of sperm-donors or surrogates and of confidentiality, but were not matters centrally concerned with infertility. Equally, the kind of research that was necessary if the techniques of IVF were to be refined, and the success-rate of the procedures improved would increase knowledge of the development of the early embryo, knowledge which could be used much more widely than in the field of infertility. (And indeed such future research came to be an increasingly important element in the discussion of the report.) How were all these aspects to be knitted together? I remember feeling a kind of fog of indecision about how to include all the issues in a coherent order. It reminded me of nothing so much as when, having done all the reading for an undergraduate essay, I was desperately trying to think how to structure it so that one element connected with another. I used sometimes to feel a kind of physical frustration at my inability to see clearly. In the end, in this case, I decided to start by listing and discussing the possible methods of 'artificial conception', whether related specifically to infertility or not, and then proceed to an exposition of the scientific issues, the development of the embryo, and the uses to which this new knowledge might be put in the future. This may not have been the ideal way to arrange things, but it meant that we could end the report with a look at issues wider than infertility itself.

In this decision-making, of central importance to anyone trying to draft a report that will be intelligible, I had enormous help from Anne. Jenny Croft's task was to try to make sense of what members of the committee said on the issues as they came up one by one, and incorporate them in the minutes. That was difficult enough to do: she had little time over for considering the structure of the report as a whole. As it was, we seemed to spend far too long debating the accuracy of these minutes. Other members of the committee, to their credit, were interested in all aspects of the material equally, none concentrating solely on the parts they already knew about (as had been the case in the construction of the report on special educational needs). Yet, understandably, they felt no responsibility for the overall shape of the report. Anne recognised the problem, and was, as usual, clear-headed, methodical and logical in her suggestions. And her drafting of the crucial paragraphs concerning the development of the embryo was impeccable. I am certain that the separation of the question of methods of treatment of infertility and the creation of new styles of family, on the one hand, from on the other the scientific issues and the possible future outcomes of the research involved, had a profound effect on our subsequent ability to get the bill that was based on the report through both houses of parliament.

Anne later joined the staff of the Wellcome Cancer Research Campaign Unit in Cambridge, and in 1991, having been elected a fellow in 1975, became the Foreign Secretary of the Royal Society, the first woman to hold office in the Society. In 2001 she was awarded the L'Oreal/UNESCO Women in Science prize, representing women in the whole of Europe. We were fortunate to have her on the committee; and after the report was published she was tireless in interpreting it, between 1984 and 1989, when the legislative process began, lecturing to MPs, schoolchildren, women's groups, as she had to us while the committee was sitting. I owe her a huge debt. She wrote to me recently that she had been an 'ethical illiterate' when she joined the committee. It had simply never struck her that, while she thought of herself as simply working on the division of cells in early mammalian development, with a view to relieving, as she said, some young healthy women from the burden of infertility, other people saw her as a murderer. The learning curve was almost as steep for her as it was for some of us, brought up as we had been in total ignorance of biological science.

In the new year of 1983, as we continued to read the huge piles of written evidence, and to take oral evidence from selected individuals and groups, the moral issues began to become clear, and we began to see where the greatest disagreements within the committee would lie, reflecting, more or less, differences of opinion within the public at large. The written evidence was, unsurprisingly, extraordinarily repetitive; I learned to skim through the submissions on the lookout for any fresh viewpoint, or, better still, fresh facts. But it was hard not to fall asleep over the papers. It was a comfort to know that the secretariat was also reading, and might pick up things that I would miss. Meanwhile, letters continued to flood in addressed to me personally, and to other committee members. As a recipient of this kind of postbag, I have just one piece of advice to offer to campaigners: always write your own letter. There is nothing more counterproductive than to receive numerous copies of an identical letter, signed, it is true by an individual, but plainly handed out from some central source. One is supposed to be impressed by the numbers of letters received. I am impressed only by the thought that has gone into them. On the whole those people who were hostile to the new techniques, and to research in the field were more likely to sign a predesigned letter than were those who were favourable to the new developments; but the numbers of each were about equal.

There were two issues concerning which it was especially difficult, indeed impossible, for the committee to agree. One of these was fundamental to the whole enterprise, and was of deep philosophical and moral interest; this was the issue which Geoffrey and I had identified when I was first asked whether I would take on the chairmanship, and which seemed to us both extremely complex and philosophically fascinating. It was the question of whether research using live human embryos in the laboratory was to be prohibited or permitted; and if permitted, was it nevertheless to be subject to mandatory regulation?

The question arose sharply for the first time in February 1983. We had taken evidence that day from the British Medical Association, who were clear in their demand that IVF, and therefore relevant research, should continue (for without further research, as they rightly argued, it could not properly be carried out). In my notes of that meeting, I remarked, 'Doctors are amazing; they cannot help making one feel grateful to them, and lucky to have the privilege of talking to them, in their inconceivably busy lives, dedicated as they are to saving us all. But I have to say they were pretty confused.' Their evidence was followed by evidence from a prominent Jesuit, Father Mahoney. He was, I recorded, superbly lucid, and I had enormous pleasure not so much in arguing with him as in making him expand what he had said at first.

I became, at this meeting, genuinely alarmed that I might be too dominant in the discussions. After all, these were philosophical issues, concerned with questions about the moral status of the human embryo in its early stages, with the origins of the unique human individual and with even broader questions about the criteria according to which such moral questions were to be answered, and about the relation between people's moral beliefs and the law. But most of the committee were profoundly uninterested in philosophy; they tended to twiddle their thumbs and gaze at the ceiling if they thought I was talking about philosophy, simply waiting until it was over, like members of my Latin classes in school-teaching days, if I started to speculate about the possible use of the subjunctive in Latin relative clauses. (The children used to wait until I'd finished and then say, 'All right; but is it or isn't it the subjunctive?' They wanted an answer, not a load of ideas.)

All this was in sharp contrast with my experience of chairing the committee of inquiry into special educational needs; and it taught me, I suppose, something about myself. It was not that I cared more about the infertile than I did about children with educational disabilities. It was simply that the intellectual problems involved in my present chairmanship were a great deal more difficult, more general, and to me far more congenial than the problems raised by the earlier inquiry. I had never before thought of myself as an intellectual, but now I began to see that perhaps I was, and must guard against the implications. At the end of this particular meeting a member of the committee who was Professor of Social and Pastoral Theology at the University of Manchester, a nice but somewhat indecisive man called Anthony Dyson, made a curious rambling speech about how all our individual professional interests were coming out, and how this might lead us into conflict. This was, I thought, provoked partly by the frequent, and to me often apparently irrelevant interventions during the day of our social worker member, Madeline Carriline, a devoted professional who found it hard to step outside her usual preoccupations, and wanted us to be mindful of 'the social work dimension'. (How could anyone, I commented afterwards, be so unselfconsciously single-track? But I should have known that they could, if I had remembered the remedial gymnasts.) However it was also partly provoked, I judged, by my own abstract and detached attitude to the issues involved. I thought the better of him for this veiled criticism. Although he constantly changed his mind (even signing a minority report which he later publicly disavowed), I came to miss his contributions when he could not attend meetings, and at least once went up to Manchester to talk to him about the 'philosophical' issues, always benefiting from our conversations.

Yet, though I now accused myself of being an intellectual, I was acutely conscious of our terms of reference, which

Some people hold that if an embryo is human and alive, it follows that it should not be deprived of a chance for development, and therefore it should not be used for research. They would give moral approval to IVF if, and only if, each embryo produced were to be transferred to a uterus. Others, while in no way denying that human embryos are alive (and they would concede that eggs and sperm are also alive), hold that embryos are not yet human persons and that if it could be decided when an embryo becomes a person, it could also be decided when it might, or might not, be permissible for research to be undertaken. Although the questions of when life or personhood begin appear to be questions of fact susceptible to straightforward answers, we hold that the answers to such questions … are complex amalgams of factual and moral judgements. Instead of trying to answer these questions directly we have therefore gone straight to the question of how it is right to treat the human embryo. We have considered what status ought to be accorded to the human embryo and the answer we give must necessarily be in terms of ethical or moral principles.

This paragraph was the most difficult to write in the whole report, and contained a philosophical point which I believed, and still believe, to be of the greatest importance, and of which I had great difficulty in persuading my colleagues. I wanted to stress the point that our question must be how we, as civilized people, ought to regard the very earliest human embryos, now for the very first time existing independently of their mothers in the laboratory, instead of in the female fallopian tube. There were some, of course, who thought that from the moment a human embryo came into existence, whether in the uterus or in the test-tube, from the 'moment of conception' as they put it, it was already, being both human and alive, deserving of protection. These people were equally opposed to abortion and to the use of embryos for research.

Some of them, as I have said, believed that it was intrinsically wrong to produce an embryo in the laboratory in the first place. These were a minority. Those who signed the dissenting note to our report, including the Roman Catholic professor, John Marshall, did not hold this extreme view. Nor did they even hold the view, outlined in our paragraph 11.9, that every embryo brought into existence in the laboratory should be placed in the uterus of the patient. They held that it was morally acceptable to fertilize eggs in the laboratory to be implanted in the uterus of a woman who could not otherwise become pregnant. But if more than the optimum number of embryos for implantation came into existence the surplus embryos should either be frozen for future implantation, or should be allowed to die. They should in no circumstances be used for research. 'Still less should embryos be deliberately created for the purpose of experimentation.'

This was a moderate, but to me rather surprising conclusion. Why should it be all right to allow some embryos to die, but not all right to use them for research before allowing them to die? In any case, that part of the dissenting opinion which seemed to authorize allowing some embryos to die seemed to be in direct contradiction with another conclusion of the same expression of dissent, which recommended that 'nothing should be done that would reduce the chance of successful implantation of the embryo'. It seemed that at least part of the objection to the use of embryos for research was the fear that if such research were allowed, even within the limitations which our report was to recommend, the limits would inevitably be breached, and experiments would run out of control. This was the 'slippery slope' argument, which has such an immense hold on people's imaginations. But such an argument should not have been necessary for those who held that it was intrinsically wrong to use human embryos for research. For those who held such a belief it was wrong to get onto the slope in the first place. I therefore felt that there was a central contradiction in John Marshall's dissenting note; but of course that was none of my business.

At any rate, the argument accepted by the majority of the committee was that we had to face the fact that a value-judgement was involved in the decision whether or not the early embryo might be used experimentally. It was for us in society to decide how we ought to regard these embryos at the very early stage of the slow process at the end of which they would undoubtedly be human babies, and might not be so used. We had no precedent here; it was vain to search the scriptures for an answer. Until our time, there had never been such a thing as a live human embryo in the laboratory, separate from its mother. To ask, as people were prone to, 'When does human life begin?' was to pose a misleading question. For it sounded like a question to which scientists could give an answer; and it was assumed by those who asked the question that if an answer was forthcoming, we would know that from that point onwards, when human life sprang into existence, the embryo was to be protected. Some members of the committee and, later, some members of parliament even begged that we might place a moratorium on research until such time as scientists could answer the question 'when does life begin?' (Frank Longford was among them.) But the trouble was that scientists would say, quite rightly, that human sperm and eggs were alive; human life does not begin with the embryo. Yet no one suggested that every spermatozoon and every egg discarded in the normal menstrual cycle should be protected from destruction. So the question being asked was not about human life, but about valuable human life. When does human life become so intrinsically valuable that it must not be destroyed, even for the sake of the good that might come from the research that would lead to its destruction? For this was the balance that had always to be kept in mind by those who did not regard the destruction of a human embryo as absolutely and intrinsically wrong.

We knew that good, not only in remedying infertility but in much wider medical outcomes, could arise out of research using early human embryos. It was this knowledge that had inspired scientists up to now, including Anne McLaren, to press on with their work. She had taught us to take a developmental view of the growth of the embryo, from the single-cell stage, to the stage when the multiplying cells were differentiated into those that would form the nervous system, the limbs, the internal organs, the skin or indeed the placenta, not a part of the embryo itself. Somewhere along this developmental line we realized that we must put up a barrier, and recommend to ministers that legislation should be introduced that would debar scientists from keeping embryos alive in the laboratory beyond this point. It could not be left to individual scientists or their teams to decide in each case how the balance between the good of the embryo and the future good to arise out of research was to be struck.

In the end, following the developmental pattern we had learned, we set the limit beyond which no embryo might be kept alive if it was still in the laboratory at fourteen days after fertilization. We chose a specific number of days because this was precise (whereas if we had chosen a point in development some embryos might have reached this point earlier or later than others). But the fourteen-day limit did correspond more or less to the time when an embryo in the uterus was likely to attach itself to the uterine wall, and when the thicker plate of cells known as the 'primitive streak' was beginning to develop within the loosely conjoined group of cells, from which eventually the central nervous system would develop. Before this had developed there was obviously no possibility that the embryo could experience anything at all, pleasurable or painful, and this was an important consideration for those hesitant about embryo research.

Another factor making fourteen days a good cut-off point was that after that time, with the development of the primitive streak, there was no longer the possibility of the cluster of cells splitting up into two clusters, to form identical twins. Thus it was difficult to argue that, before that time, there was one identifiable human being, which could be traced as one, from conception through birth to death. This was much the same argument as was later used by a Salesian priest, a member of a Roman Catholic order in Melbourne, Dr Norman Ford, who was concerned to overturn the theory of the beginning of individuality, or personal identity, which had been adapted from Aristotle by Aquinas, and accepted as the orthodoxy of the Roman Catholic Church.* Ford rejected the doctrine that human life begins at conception, preferring to distinguish between life and morally significant or strictly individual life. Even though all the genetic material which goes to make up a single embryo or two identical twin embryos was present in the single cell brought into being by

---

* See Norman M. Ford, *When Did I Begin?* (Cambridge: Cambridge University Press, 1988).

the fertilization of the egg, he argued that this was not enough to make that single cell an individual person. That must come later, when the cells have multiplied and have begun to differentiate into the different types of cell that would make up the organism as it grew. I met Dr Ford, and had several conversations with him when I was in Australia in 1985. I greatly admired his courage in writing his book, which was of course rejected by the Roman Catholic Church.

Thus there were several reasons which together made us decide to place the limit of embryo research at fourteen days; there was the need to have a precise and definite limit, to reassure the public that no scientist could continue down the slippery slope, to the end-point when research would be permitted on developed fetuses or babies (and for this reason we recommended that to keep an embryo alive longer than fourteen days should be a criminal offence); there was the consideration that no embryo before that time (and probably for much longer) could possibly be thought to suffer; and there was the thought that there was no individual human being in existence before that time, although all the genetic material that would ultimately make up the individual or individuals was in place.

We were much criticized for this amalgam of arguments. We were told, most oddly, in my view, that there could be one human being even if, later, this human being developed two bodies, and became two organisms.* This argument would entail that identical twins were one human being. This seems to me a totally incoherent view. Identical twins may share the same genome; but an organism is not nothing

---

* See, for example, Michael Lockwood, 'The Warnock Report: A Philosophical Appraisal', in M. Lockwood (ed.), *Modern Medicine* (Oxford: Oxford University Press, 1985).

but its genes; and there can be no possible doubt that identical twins are two organisms. They are, after all, spatially and geographically separate. We were told that the pre-fourteen-day embryo was potentially a human being, and therefore must not be used for research any more than may an actual human being, without consent. This seems to me just another way of restating the Roman Catholic view that what is human is equally to be valued at whatever stage of its development. We were told that it was impossible to know for certain that a pre-fourteen-day embryo could not suffer. This seems to me simply false. Before the development of a central nervous system, it is physiologically impossible for there to exist human experience of any kind. Finally, and most frequently, we were told that the cut-off point was arbitrary. Of course, in one sense it was, in that it might have been fixed at thirteen days or at fifteen days. But, as I have said, there were good reasons for fixing it at about that time; and it was essential to have some cut-off point or other. I still find myself irritated by comments like that of David Galton, who, complaining about the injustice and unimaginative nature of law in the UK, wrote:

> If you undertake experiments on an embryo older than fourteen days you can expect to be treated like a criminal and serve a prison sentence, whereas if the embryo is less than fourteen days old you are treated as a bona fide research scientist. No wonder such ruling is in danger of receiving such little public trust as to make it ineffective.*

---

* David Galton, *In Our Own Image* (New York: Little, Brown & Co., 2001), p. 163.

This seems to me a pretty fatuous comment. You might as well argue that it is unjust and unimaginative to prevent someone travelling abroad if his passport is one day out of date. The law cannot be flexible in such matters. Someone who keeps an embryo alive for longer than the statutory limit can obviously 'expect to be treated like a criminal'. Such a person has in fact committed a criminal offence. (Moreover, I know of no evidence to show that the law is ineffective.)

In the paper quoted above, Michael Lockwood* put forward a plausible argument to show that we should have set the time limit on research considerably later than fourteen days. We did discuss this possibility. In rejecting it, I was made aware of an absolutely central consideration in the work of such committees as ours. This was the difference between what one might personally think was sensible, or even morally right, and what is most likely to be acceptable as a matter of public policy. Obvious though this point is, I think I was very slow to grasp it, and some members of the committee never grasped it. On this particular issue, it became clear that we needed to set a limit which would allow for some research, but which nevertheless would satisfy anyone who thought about it that individual embryos would not be subjected to suffering. This would still have been true, if we had set a later limit. But it was essential to be seen to err on the side of extreme caution. Time and again we found ourselves distinguishing not between what would be right or wrong, but between what would be acceptable or unacceptable. At first, when Jenny used such language in her drafts, I used to take out the word 'acceptable', mentally accusing her of being mealy-mouthed, too timid to use full-

---

* Lockwood, 'The Warnock Report'.

blooded words like 'wrong' – but in fact I realised she was probably right. It very slowly dawned on me that, though the issues with which we were concerned were undoubtedly moral issues, and though the private sentiments of individual members of the committee in some cases ran very high, our task was not to express our feelings, it was to try to assemble a coherent policy which might seem, if not right, then at least all right, to the largest possible number of people. For we had very early, and without difficulty, decided that in certain areas, and especially in the area of research, it was going to be necessary for parliament to introduce primary legislation. I knew quite well, even from the experience of our own committee, let alone from all the written and oral evidence we received, that our moral differences were not capable of resolution, at least not on the central issue of research. If, as we all did, we wanted to allow the medical progress that had been made to continue, we had to hope that parliament would accept our major recommendations, not as perfect, but as reasonable and not unduly offensive to people's moral feelings. We had to hope, that is to say, to achieve a broad consensus about what could be tolerated, even by those who would have preferred prohibition to regulation.

I learned that the language of 'right' and 'wrong' was inflammatory; that it sounded arrogant, and that it provoked conflict. The very best one could hope for was to find something roughly 'acceptable'. And in the end, even those on the committee who had submitted dissenting opinions nevertheless signed the report. Our task had been to recommend a policy which might allow the sort of medical and scientific progress which was in the public interest, while at the same time not riding roughshod over the moral scruples of a significant number of the public. We were not asking people to give up their moral scruples, in so far as these affected themselves. No one who thought that research using human embryos was wrong was being asked, still less compelled, to take part in it, any more than those who disapprove of the use of animals in the laboratory are compelled to use them, or those who are entirely opposed to abortion are compelled to submit to it. What we were asking was that our recommendations should be laid before parliament; and if parliament so decided, people should accept the legislation democratically proposed, without sacrificing their own right to continue to lobby to have the law changed.

Plainly, those who were opposed to the use of embryos for research believed not only that they themselves should not use them, but that no one should; if something is wrong, it is wrong for anyone. Moreover, for most people, the question whether they should or should not personally engage in embryo research does not arise. But those who are opposed to it believe that it is wrong that anyone should so engage; and they would prefer to live in a society where such things did not occur. Yet in matters of legislation, it is impossible to avoid consequentialist arguments: What will come of a policy, for good or ill? The question must be one of weighing up future good against the possible outrage of moral feelings (for, if our recommendations were accepted, and embryos were not to be kept alive for longer than fourteen days from fertilization, there would be no question of any suffering of the embryos to be weighed in the balance). In this case, the moral outrage, though strongly felt, did not, as it turned out, represent a consensus. I had never been so conscious of the difference between considerations of private morality and those of the common good, nor of the absolute requirement of democracy that the common good must be the goal, difficult though it may be to discern it.

This is not to say that all reports must be so pragmatic, or so bent on consensus, or 'the acceptable'. Sometimes reports are produced which call attention to scandals that have been perpetrated, or are still being perpetrated, or where positive evil has been uncovered, which could not possibly be acceptable, and indeed where part of the scandal is that the evil has been unthinkingly accepted. I hope that if I were the Chief Inspector of Prisons, obliged to report to government, I should use the strong language that both the last two Chief Inspectors, Stephen Tumim and David Ramsbotham, used. They were reporting on what was a moral scandal; and in bringing to the attention of government and the public at large the state of the institutions where young offenders were incarcerated, they were pointing out a manifest evil which could also have none but disastrous consequences. Public policy and individual outrage surely here coincided.

Our report was of a different order. We were trying to advise government about how wholly new and unfamiliar creatures, namely live human embryos fertilized in the laboratory, ought in future to be regarded. In most people's eyes, nothing immoral had been done in bringing such creatures into the world. It was a matter of looking into the future, and trying to see how public benefit could be combined with a reasonable reassurance that no moral scandals would follow.

The second issue which divided the committee was of far less fundamental significance. This was the issue of surrogate mothers. At the time that we were meeting, commercial agencies for the supply of surrogates were springing up in America, and some were poised to set up branches in the UK – indeed someone called Mrs Quinton had already begun to advertise both for potential surrogates and for couples who wanted to use the service. There are two main forms of surrogacy. The most usual is where a woman is infertile, and her husband's sperm is used to inseminate by AID another woman who will give birth to the baby and hand it over, according to a contract. The other case is where a woman can produce eggs but cannot sustain a pregnancy (or her health would be endangered if she did). In this case her eggs and her husband's sperm are fertilized *in vitro*, and the resulting embryo is placed in the uterus of the surrogate. This has the advantage that the parents who receive the baby when it is born are both the genetic parents of the baby; but the probability of a successful outcome is less, because of the comparatively low success-rate (even now) of IVF. The surrogate also has to undergo a far more complicated procedure than the relatively simple procedure of AID.

We should have been able to reach agreement fairly easily on what we would recommend about surrogacy, and I have to say that it was largely my fault that we argued about it endlessly, and had constantly to come back to it, when we should have been discussing quite different issues. And, while on the matter of the moral status of the early embryo I probably seemed, as I have said, too 'philosophical' or detached, on this issue I might properly have been accused of being too emotional, not to say irrational. I felt a very strong abhorrence of surrogacy, and I should not have allowed this to influence me as it did. And because this was a matter of feeling rather than reason, I was unable to set out any very coherent arguments for my position, which was that surrogacy should be prohibited. I was not alone in these feelings. Indeed, everyone agreed that the practice would very often end in the courts, if a woman who had sustained the pregnancy and given birth then changed her mind, and refused to hand over the baby. Moreover, there was a general feeling that it was morally wrong that a commercial agency should make money out of the sometimes desperate desire of a couple to have a child; and that on the other side there was a risk of impoverished women being exploited by such agencies.

My strong feelings I think arose from two sources. The first was my own sentimental view of childbirth. I was so far from being able to imagine handing over a baby to whom I had given birth, so keenly able to remember the bliss of seeing this new life, that I immediately felt it to be morally outrageous that anyone should contract before the pregnancy began that she would hand over the baby. The second reason was that I was offended by the kind of language used by people involved, as agents or as surrogates, in the procedure. There were agents who spoke of forcing surrogate mothers to keep their contract and hand over the baby, even if they pleaded to keep it; on the other side there were women who spoke of becoming a surrogate in order to pay for a new carpet for the sitting-room. Both seemed to degrade the phenomenon of pregnancy and childbirth. I was appalled, too, on a visit to New York, where I was interviewed by a reporter who had just visited a new surrogacy agency, and was slavering with enthusiasm about the wonderful pictures on the walls of the office of the luscious girls he could have chosen, if he had been looking for a surrogate.

But my distaste was, surely, more a matter of aesthetics than of morals. I generally tried to act on the principle that disliking something, or feeling queasy about it was not sufficient ground for declaring that it should be prohibited. Indeed I used to become irritated when members of the committee said that 'they were not happy' about something, and failed to be able or willing to go further, and uncover the reason for their unhappiness. I was once reduced to saying crossly to Jean Walker, the wife of the Bishop of Ely, 'We are

103

not brought into this world to be happy.' But on the issue of surrogacy, I was no better.

Moreover, in general I believed that it was far better to try to regulate than to prohibit, since prohibition generally led to a continuation of the practice in question, under the worst possible conditions, and those who signed the expression of dissent about surrogacy proposed a form of regulation, not unlike the regulation of adoption, which now seems to me eminently sensible. I undoubtedly antagonized both the signatories, Dr Davies and Dr Wendy Greengross. She was a GP with whom on other grounds I did not get on very well, because she was always demanding that we take longer over our deliberations, and that we should not aim to meet our deadline, claiming, in my view hopelessly, that we could present a unanimous report if only we took longer. And at very last meeting, in early June of 1984, her ally, David Davies, was saying 'What's so sacred about June 26th?' (This was the day we on which we had agreed to hand over the report, the press conference had been called, and everyone had adjusted their diaries accordingly.) In any case, I blame myself for failing to recognize the good sense of this minority report; I should have urged that it be adopted as the recommendation of the committee.

Another source of (this time minor) disagreement among committee members was the concept of counselling. On a visit to Belfast at some stage of our deliberations we put to a group of doctors the question of whether they thought that some couples asking for infertility treatment should be refused it on social rather than clinical grounds. We had discussed this matter at some length among ourselves, and had invented a couple with a known record of child abuse. Should the consultant proceed with the treatment? Dame Josephine Barnes had shocked us by stating that if she thought a couple were unsuitable to bring up children, she refused them treatment, telling them that in doing so she was exercising her clinical judgement. This solution did not find favour, and in the end we recommended that if a consultant refused to treat a couple, they must be told the grounds of the rejection.

At any rate, there was a voluble gynaecologist in Belfast who answered the question by saying that in such a case he would counsel the couple. I said, 'But what would you do if they persisted in asking for treatment?', to which he replied, 'I would counsel them and counsel them until they went away.' I liked this answer, because it seemed to me to illustrate the difficulty there was in attaching any precise meaning to the word 'counselling'. Some people thought it meant simply giving the facts about a particular procedure, including any risks it might carry, the normal exchange of information that all doctors give their patients. Others thought it meant giving advice, an interpretation rejected by our social worker member, Madeline Carriline, and by the one-time student counsellor, Jean Walker. They held that counselling, properly so called, was entirely value-free. And yet they believed it to be more than mere informing. It had a therapeutic function. What this was, I never quite discovered. Jean Walker once said, 'I'm sorry you have this problem about counselling.' I replied, of course, that it wasn't a problem so much as a degree of scepticism, or simple confusion. In whatever way we variously understood the term, we put among our recommendations that counselling should be available to patients at fertility clinics, avoiding Madeline Carriline's demand that patients should be obliged to receive it, by law. So no great harm came of the ambiguities of the concept.

We had another memorable residential meeting in Cardiff, in March 1984, which is illustrative of the conditions in which we worked in those days. Mindful of the horrors of the Llandaff College where the committee on special educational needs had met, I made sure that we stayed in a hotel this time; so we stayed in a Holiday Inn, outside the city. There was hot water, and excessive but perfectly edible food.

We were well into the process of drafting the report by now; and it was of no use to say, as people frequently do, that you cannot draft with a whole committee sitting round the table. Since every member will object to some words or other in a draft, it is absolutely essential that, on key issues, a draft shall be constructed and agreed at the table. The difficulty was in getting things down on paper so that everyone could scrutinize them. Fortunately the hotel had a photocopier. But no one had a typewriter; and, as it soon emerged, not one of the three members of the secretariat who were present, Jeremy Metters, Jenny Croft and her nice, clever assistant, Elizabeth Lynam, could type. This surprised me at first, until I remembered that on joining the upper grade of the Civil Service you were advised not to learn to type, and to conceal the ability to do so if you had it, on the grounds that it might come to be expected that you would do your own typing, which would be unfitting for your status.

So how were we to produce bits of the draft that could be read and agreed on the spot? If we could not do this, progress would be vastly delayed. Ken Rawnsley, a professor at Cardiff University, volunteered to collect his typewriter from his office, and I volunteered to type the things we thought we had agreed, copy them and table them. So each lunch-break, in the time between the end of our meetings and dinner, and far into the night, I sat collating the notes made by Jenny and Elizabeth and turning them into continuous prose for members to scrutinize and agree. The hotel even managed to find me a little room with a decent table to work at, though it had the drawback of being unheated and next to the bar, which made it both uncomfortable and noisy.

The last part of our agenda at this long exhausting meeting, to be tackled on the final morning, was a return to the dread subject of surrogacy, which we had left unfinished because we knew that Callum McNaughton, who had been away in Australia and was now back, had wanted a loophole left for consultants to arrange surrogacy for their patients, as a matter of last resort. We had therefore postponed further discussion until what had come to be known as McNaughton's Loophole could be expounded. (In the event, he had changed his mind, and no longer wanted a loophole of any kind.) As ill-luck would have it, the hotel management had not realized that we had scheduled a meeting for that morning, and had given up our room to another conference. We were obliged to meet in the bar.

It was the most disastrous meeting. I had never before realized how crucial to the proper conduct of business is a table, and upright chairs. (I remembered afterwards that in the 1950s, the philosopher J. L. Austin had always wanted his Saturday morning discussions to take place in such a setting, on the grounds that no one could think without a hard chair and a table.) Everyone, including me, was bad-tempered. People interrupted each other, no one addressed their remarks to the chairman; it was pandemonium. We still had surrogacy as unfinished business when people began to drift off home. I was acutely miserable. Only kind-hearted Ken Rawnsley said that I had managed as well as anyone could; but I did not believe him. Even Jenny was silent. It was certainly a bad note on which to end; there seemed no hope of progress, nothing but endless arguments which went round and round in circles, everyone convinced of the irrationality of his or her colleagues. I felt thoroughly ashamed.

It is difficult now to believe what obstacles lay in the path of committee work in those days. We never got our papers until the very last minute, sometimes not until after the meeting they referred to. I once asked Jenny how this could be, and she told me that the DHSS was very short of typists in the typing pool, and everything had to be sent to Scunthorpe to be typed. (Why Scunthorpe, I never knew.) As, for a part of the life of the committee, there was a postal strike, the delays were not to be wondered at. I was told, on asking, that there was one computer in the DHSS, and that though we could book time on it if we liked, that was hardly worth doing because it had to be at the disposal of the Minister, and so a booking for a particular date was likely to be cancelled. It was not surprising that, as time went on, nerves were frayed.

From the next month after our Cardiff meeting I was allocated a little office in the DHSS, which actually had a window, though it looked out onto a pretty squalid scene. There I worked with Jenny and Jeremy for long and on the whole peaceful hours on the final draft. Meetings of the committee were less and less enjoyable. One hot day in our windowless box the air-conditioning failed. Members, through no fault of their own, did not attend regularly. Ken Rawnsley was ill, suffering from incurable cancer, as it turned out. Our two legal members were mostly tied up in court. Apart from those who still called for more time, there was a spirit of resignation. We knew that we could not reach agreement on the crucial issue of embryo research – that had been clear from the beginning: no one could suppose that John Marshall, a man of high intelligence combined with deep conviction, would compromise his principle of the sanctity of the life of potential human beings. We also knew that other issues, whether agreed or not, were of lesser importance. Only one firm determination came out of these final meetings: that the establishing of a new statutory licensing authority to regulate both research and infertility treatment should be the first of our recommendations. That this was accepted by government, so that even before the authority could be set up by law, an interim regulatory body was immediately brought into being, was perhaps the most immediate beneficial result of our report. I was thankful, at any rate, that we all signed the report, and that no one had resigned from the committee.

The day of publication, and the handing-over ceremony was a muted affair compared with the jollification after the report on special needs had been handed over. I, as it happened, had been with Geoffrey to an extremely delicious lunch with Norman St John Stevas, as he then was. He was cultivating Geoffrey at the time, partly because he wanted a protégé to be admitted to Oxford as an undergraduate, and thought that Geoffrey might be able to help; and partly because he was himself beginning to hanker for a job as head of a college, and again thought that the Vice-Chancellor would be a good contact. (Later, when the protégé failed to get an Oxford place, he wrote me a postcard, saying that he had 'gone off' Geoffrey. He himself became a spectacular and generous Master of Emmanuel College, Cambridge, quite without anybody's influence.) On this occasion Princess Margaret was one of the guests, and she arrived extremely late, and then had to be given time for several glasses of gin and cigarettes before lunch could be served. (The cigarettes, of course, continued, between every course.) I began to be anxious about whether I would get away by the time I was supposed to be at Elephant and Castle to sign and hand over the report, and I have little recollection of the conversation, because of this mounting panic. Fortunately Geoffrey had his driver waiting to take him back to Oxford in the Vice-Chancellor's car, so I was driven fast and expertly to the DHSS, and arrived just in time.

There had been many reproaches from the Department, and even from the Minister, about the leaks that had been appearing in *The Times*, so in my little speech of thanks and farewell, with Norman Fowler still present, I apologized for these leaks, and said that the secretariat was entirely blameless in the matter. This caused a bit of a frisson, but I felt that it had to be said. I got on extremely well with Norman Fowler at this ceremony, who was cheerful because of the birth of a son almost the day before, and he asked me to give him a tutorial about the issues, at some later date. This I did, with great pleasure on my side. After he had left, we all shuffled off, probably glad to be rid of each other. The only person of whom I took a proper farewell was Ken Rawnsley, who in fact did not live for very long after this time. I continued to see Callum McNaughton from time to time, and when I went to Glasgow in the spring of 1992 to deliver the Gifford Lectures at the university, he was wonderfully hospitable, and loyal in attending the lectures with his GP daughter. I also continued to see Anne McLaren, with whom I sometimes shared a platform, in the years between the publication of the report and the legislation that came out of it in 1990. Otherwise the committee had done its job punctually, and very properly faded into the past. I shall postpone discussion of the outcomes and the swift advances in science that came afterwards until the next chapter.

# 3 Genetics

Since 1984, when the Committee of Inquiry into Human Fertility and Embryology reported, there have been enormous advances in biotechnology. Though the success rate of IVF has not improved as much as was hoped (it seems to remain at about 20 per cent, though an average figure is not really informative: there are great differences between the success rate at different clinics; and the younger the woman seeking treatment, the greater are her chances of a successful outcome), yet the whole field of embryology has expanded. It is now concerned with far wider issues than fertility and infertility. Nearly all the new developments and hoped-for medical applications of the new technologies depend, nevertheless, on IVF, so research designed to make this a more uniformly successful procedure still continues, and, though perhaps not the most glamorous, is still one of the most important areas of research.

Moving beyond IVF itself, in Chapter 12 of the 1984 report, entitled 'Possible Future Developments in Research', we foresaw, to a certain extent, the interest that was going to develop in genetic manipulation, in the production of genetically modified human embryos and in cloning, as it was then envisaged. We tried, in our report, to avoid the pitfall of failure to foresee the developments that we knew

111

lay ahead, and equally the pitfall of excessive speculation that would draw us into the world of science fiction. It was because we recognized that things were on the brink of an explosion in the knowledge of human genetics that we insisted, as our first priority, on the establishing of a statutory body that would keep developments under review and issue licences for all research in the field. But the great problem, the status of the human embryo in the laboratory, would undoubtedly remain at the centre of controversy. And, although we did not know it, and could not have known it at the time, another problem was going to arise. There would emerge, during the next fifteen years, the possibility, the real possibility, that a human embryo might be created not merely outside the human body, by the fertilizing of a human egg in the laboratory, but asexually, by cell nuclear transfer, rather than by fertilization of any kind. The human involvement in the making of embryos would seem to have been even further put to one side. Such issues as these have become the centre of the controversies at the beginning of the twenty-first century. It is the gradual emergence of these issues that is the subject of this chapter.

After the flurry of media excitement that followed the publication of the Report of the Committee of Inquiry on Human Fertilization and Embryology in 1984, things went very quiet. There was, at any rate, little reaction from any government source. It was not particularly quiet for me personally. After the first rush of interviews and television programmes, I was fairly constantly asked to give talks and lectures, to undergraduates, parliamentarians and lawyers, among others, about the issues involved. Anne Maclaren, who had, as I have said, been a most indispensable and authoritative member of the committee, often joined me on various platforms to explain the facts, and our view of the ethics, of the early development of the human embryo. Of course she was far more knowledgeable than I, and was able to exert on this wider audience the clarity and charm of manner with which members of the committee had become familiar. The level of public understanding of the issues rose, at least a bit.

Before the end of 1984, I was commissioned by Blackwell publishers to produce a volume that would incorporate the whole report with a new introduction, explaining the philosophical ideas that underpinned it. It was published in 1985, under the title *A Question of Life*.* This was not particularly difficult to do; it was a matter of expanding what was in the report, and clarifying in my own mind what had been the arguments for our main conclusion, that research using human embryos should be permitted but regulated. But I came in for a good deal of criticism from some of the more discontented members of the former committee for consenting to the publication of this book. In particular, David Davies, never friendly, wrote to complain that the proceeds of the book were not going to be distributed among committee members. After all, they had all contributed to the report. I was genuinely astonished. I was able to reply that I had been paid the sum of £100 by Blackwells for the introduction (to which the committee had not contributed); and that otherwise there were no profits from the book at all, the copyright for the report itself lying with the Controller of Her Majesty's Stationery Office. I did not hear from him again.

I also undertook a series of articles for women's magazines, and helped launch a questionnaire in, I think,

---

* Mary Warnock, *A Question of Life* (Oxford: Basil Blackwell, 1985).

*Woman's Own*, to ascertain the views of women in the non-academic world. I greatly enjoyed both the quite taxing task of putting together the questionnaire, with the help of a professional sociologist who worked in the field of opinion polls, and analysing the answers. On the whole the respondents were strongly in favour of permitting research to go forward which would alleviate the problems of infertility; but some of those same people expressed doubts about the use of live human embryos for research. I began to feel that our report, with its minority dissenting opinion, reflected almost exactly the state of public opinion among those who were interested.

In addition to all this, there were European conferences. It was recognized that IVF had been pioneered in this country, and that legislation to regulate it was likely to start here. I had, for example, an enormously enjoyable visit to Venice for a conference on the subject. (I was put up in the Danieli Hotel. But, alas, my visit coincided with a strike of all the hotel staff; so there was no hot water, no heating, no meals in the restaurant; no one cleaned my room or made my bed. It was, in fact, the most amazingly uncomfortable stay in any hotel I have ever had. The thought of all the illustrious past visitors to the hotel, though intellectually exciting, did little to compensate for the physical privations.) In Venice I met the clever sensible scientific correspondent of the *Observer*, Robin McKie, and came to understand what an important role serious scientific journalists had, and would in future have, in informing public opinion about the new, rapidly advancing, technologies in the biological sciences. Their role in the interpretation of articles in professional scientific journals, for readers of broadsheet newspapers, has not diminished; indeed as this country becomes more and more obsessed with health, it has greatly increased.

114

The best spin-off for me was an invitation to Melbourne, to receive an honorary degree, and to give a series of lectures on bioethics at Ormond College. I had never been to Australia before, and had always wanted to go. Geoffrey, when it was known that he was coming over, was asked to give lectures as well, mostly in Monash University, also in Melbourne, where the notorious defender of the rights of animals Peter Singer then ran a department of medical ethics. So we spent a hugely enjoyable two months, July and August 1986, staying in a flat in Ormond College, doing our shopping in the Italian quarter of the city, and, when we had time, seeing the country and enjoying wonderful hospitality. I look back on it as an extremely happy time, even though I was under great pressure, almost amounting to persecution from a lawyer and rabbi called Waller, who was heading an inquiry for the State of Victoria that was the equivalent of our 1984 committee, and which was hardening against the use of embryos for research (or at least the chairman was).

We worked quite hard, but were also lavishly entertained by the charming New Zealander, a graduate in English from Oxford, who was Principal of Ormond College (and who went back to New Zealand to fish whenever he had a spare weekend), and also by the governor-general. We were taken for great walks to see the wildlife in Anarky Park by members of the college, invited to the opera and taken to see the penguins by the parents of a charming Australian fellow of Girton, a chemist, who lived in Melbourne. It was a perfect mixture of work and social life. I fell in love with Melbourne, and with Australia in general, and I long to go back.

All this activity formed the background to my starting as Mistress of Girton in January 1985, and to a good deal of family activity, children's weddings and Geoffrey's impending retirement as Principal of Hertford College, Oxford, in the autumn of 1988. People frequently asked me whether I did not feel angry that the government was sitting on our report on embryology and doing nothing. I was in fact, at first, glad of the time, and thought that it was usefully deployed in getting people to understand the issues, as far as possible. Later I was so busy with other things that I more or less forgot it. But I never seriously doubted that eventually a bill would come before parliament that would incorporate at least some of our recommendations; and in the meantime the recommendation that had been at the top of our list, that 'A new statutory licensing authority be established to regulate both research and those infertility services which we have recommended should be subject to control' had been implemented, as far as was possible before legislation, by the establishment of an 'interim' body to undertake licensing and inspection of fertility services and research establishments. This body worked extremely hard, fitting in their obligations with their other work for no remuneration. It may well have been their inability to keep up with the work-load that finally galvanized the government to set in motion a bill, to start in the House of Lords, aiming to put into effect our remaining recommendations.

The other consideration that at last made further delay undesirable to government was that there was increasing pressure from a group called the Society for the Protection of Unborn Children for legislation that would prohibit all research using human embryos, and thus bring to an end not only IVF, but any further advance in the increasingly important field of early embryonic development and genetic manipulation.

In 1985 Enoch Powell had brought forward a private member's bill, the Unborn Child (protection) Bill seeking to impose a ban on all research. This bill did not succeed, though at report stage it gained a majority in the House of Commons of 157 to 82, but then fell, through shortage of time, some said by means of disgraceful filibustering tactics on the part of its opponents. Although it was generally thought unlikely that government would bring forward legislation before the general election, scheduled for the summer of 1987, there was due to be a ballot for private member's bills in November 1986, and it was thought that there were well over 60 MPs anxious to reintroduce Enoch Powell's Unborn Child (protection) Bill.

This bill had aroused deep passion on both sides. But, by now, those who were most strongly in favour of research were not so much interested in improving the chances of the infertile as in the possibility of genetic manipulation at the early embryonic stage, to remove or replace a faulty gene that would be responsible for a genetic disease if it were allowed to remain. For this was where the excitement and the new technology lay. Enormous advances were being made in the techniques involved in isolating human genes, and the international plan to map the complete human genome, the map of all the genes in the human organism, was being undertaken. It was already possible to isolate human genes and study their individual function in cells.

There was therefore considerable optimism, and a widespread belief that gene therapy could lead to the elimination of some common monogenetic diseases, such as cystic fibrosis, if research were allowed to continue. In those days many people, both among MPs and the general public, who were most in favour of embryonic research were themselves disabled or were closely involved with those who were. For example, during the heated debate on the Enoch Powell bill, a Welsh MP, Dafydd Wigley, who had lost two children through a congenital disease, became so enraged that he broke the arm of the Speaker's chair. It seemed highly probable that such scenes would be re-enacted, and that a bill might get through that was ill-considered and hasty, if government did not take action on our report. Nothing of the kind in fact occurred, but by the time the 1987 election was over, even I, though redoubling my efforts to explain the content of the report to whoever would listen, began to wish for time to be found for a bill to implement the recommendations. And the scientific and medical professions were becoming openly impatient, and highly critical of the continuing delay. A White Paper was published in the autumn of 1987, and there was widespread consultation. It was plain that something was going to happen at last.

The government bill was finally published in November 1989, and it came to its second reading, for debate, on 7 December. Though I had been appointed to the House of Lords, as a crossbencher, in 1985, I very seldom had time to go there during this period, and I still felt a newcomer and intimidated. I had spoken a few times, never with pleasure, and never, I thought, getting it right. (I am still not good at it, being inclined to overcomplicated argument and to a manner too reminiscent of the lecture-room, perhaps too ironic and not sufficiently declamatory, or visionary. Crossbenchers have either to bring real expertise to their speeches, or an individual persuasiveness, if they are to get members of the House to take them seriously. They carry, after all, no specifically political weight. I had neither professional expertise, nor charisma.)

However, on this occasion, I felt I had to speak, though briefly. Brevity was proper because I believed that I had already put my arguments in favour of embryo research as

118

clearly and publicly as I could. Moreover I would be in grave danger of that peculiarly irritating response 'She would say that, wouldn't she?' if I spoke up for implementing the conclusions of the report. In any case, no one would want to hear a load of philosophical arguments about the particular and different status that should be accorded to the embryo before fourteen days from fertilization. For it was quite plain from the beginning that this was to be the decisive issue.

But there was much else in the bill, especially about the new statutory authority, and about the regulation of fertility treatment apart from IVF itself (which could hardly proceed if research using live embryos were to be prohibited), which I hoped would not be lost, even if the vote went against research.

The Lord Chancellor, Lord McKay of Clashfern, introduced the bill in a long and totally admirable speech, setting out all the issues with the greatest clarity. When he came to the issue of research he explained that the bill as it stood contained two alternative clauses, Clause 11a and Clause 11b, one of which proposed that research using human embryos should be prohibited, the other that it should be prohibited save only for research carried out earlier than fourteen days from fertilization. Then there was an agreeably lawyer-like Clause 11c, saying that 11a and 11b could not both be passed. By this somewhat unusual drafting, it was made possible for people to vote unambiguously on this one issue, while probably leaving the rest of the bill, for what it would then be worth, intact.

By the time it came for me to speak, I was, most unusually for me, manifestly and suddenly suffering from flu, which my secretary at Girton already had. I was freezing cold and shivering, and had almost entirely lost my voice. My speech was even less of a success than usual. Fortunately, hardly anyone could hear it.

During the course of the series of debates on the bill at committee stage, there were several notable speeches. One of the most influential was that from the then Archbishop of York, Dr John Habgood, a lapsed biological scientist. He argued that, scientifically speaking, there was not a single 'moment of conception' at which, as the Roman Catholic Church claims, the soul enters the body and a human person comes into existence. One should, he said, regard the embryo, from the two-cell stage onwards developmentally, as biologists habitually do, becoming gradually more and more of a human person. Christians, he said, were no more bound to believe in a single moment of conception at which a human person springs into existence than they were bound to believe in Adam and Eve and the Garden of Eden. A Darwinian gradualism has replaced both myths. He was therefore in favour of research using the very early embryo because of the medical good that could come of it. This speech caused something of a frisson among certain fundamentalist Christians. An aged neighbour on the crossbenches later told me that no Christian could possibly accept research using human embryos, before or after fourteen days. I said, 'But what about the Archbishop of York?'; to which he replied '*He's* not a Christian.' I did not argue.

The other highly influential speech was from John Walton, Lord Walton of Detchant, who had only very recently become a member of the House of Lords, and who spoke passionately about the possibilities, though probably not, he said, for ten or twenty years, of genetic diagnosis and gene-replacement in embryos before implantation. He used as his main example the possibility of preventing babies being born suffering from Duchenne's muscular dystrophy, the disease in which he, as a neurologist, had specialized. He also revealed that he was a lay reader in the Methodist Church, whose view of the issue of research was about to be published. The Methodists agreed with the view put forward, though in a personal capacity, by the Archbishop of York.

The crucial clause permitting research using human embryos up to fourteen days from fertilization was passed by a substantial majority. After an exceptionally long third reading debate, the bill was finally passed by the House of Lords, where it had started, and sent on to the House of Commons on 20 March 1990. But our troubles were by no means over.

When the Human Fertilization and Embryology Bill came back to the House of Lords from the Commons, on 18 October 1990, it came with an amendment to insert a new clause at the end of the bill which was nothing whatever to do with the regulation of fertility treatments and research using human embryos, but which was in effect an amendment to the Abortion Act of 1967, seeking to lower the time of gestation at which an abortion might legally be carried out to 24 weeks, rather than 28. The justification for this change was the increased possibility, through advances in neonatal medicine, of a baby's being able to survive if it was born as early as 24, or even 22 weeks. However, it was proposed that there should be certain exceptions to the limit of 24 weeks. The amendment proposed that the upper time-limit should not apply when termination would save a woman's life, or prevent serious and permanent damage to her health, or where the fetus was found to be so damaged that if the child were born, it would suffer 'from such physical or mental abnormalities as to be seriously handicapped'.

Those of us who were anxious for the Fertilization and Embryology Bill to succeed were seriously alarmed by the addition of this Commons amendment. There had been deep controversy about abortion ever since the subject first came before parliament, many years before. To avoid becoming enmeshed in further controversy, the committee of inquiry had been expressly told to keep the subject of fertilization completely separate from that of abortion (though we did add one footnote to the effect that legislation might be needed to bring control over the use for research purposes of live fetuses which were the result of abortion into line with our recommendation that there should be no use of embryos beyond fourteen days from fertilization).

Many people thought that the 1967 Act was too permissive: the amendment tacked onto the bill and passed in the House of Commons seemed to be going still further, though admittedly only in exceptional cases. The 'pro-life' group took exception to the suggestion that any abortion should be carried out later than 24 weeks, and they were especially hostile to the proposal that the gross deformity of the fetus should be a ground for abortion.

I cannot here recount the whole story of the attempts to change the law on abortion (or the related but totally confused and otiose Infant Life Preservation Act of 1929, which although really not concerned with abortion at all, but with infanticide, was frequently cited by the pro-life party, since it made use of the dubious concept of the viability of the fetus). But in summary, since 1969 there had been four private bills introduced in the House of Lords, seeking to amend the 1967 Abortion Act, and eight private members' bills in the House of Commons, all of which had been extensively debated, but none of which had succeeded, for lack of time. It may have seemed to some that to tack an amendment onto a bill that was well on its way to being enacted might be a way to achieve reform. Government was powerless either to press for its acceptance or to refuse to allow it, since a free, non-party vote had been promised on every aspect of the bill. Whatever the motivation had been for introducing the amendment now, it was going to be used as a last-ditch attempt by the pro-life opponents of research using live embryos to ensure that the amendment would be turned down by the House of Lords and the whole bill would thus be lost. This at least was the way I saw it. Indirectly, it was a wrecking amendment. The Lord Chancellor warned of this. He said

> Whatever view one takes on these highly sensitive and controversial issues ... there is I believe a broad consensus about the need for legislation on embryo research so that it can be brought under statutory control. Noble Lords need no reminder from me that a condition for a bill to reach the statute book is that this House and another place agree on the content of the bill on the basis of the procedure which has been followed. If there were to be any persistent disagreement between the two Houses on this amendment that process would be put in jeopardy. If that occurred and there were no bill there would be no legislative control at all over embryo research and related subjects.

I have seldom felt more pessimistic.

The only ground for hope was that in the summer a private bill had been introduced by Lord Houghton of Sowerby, a fiercely combative 90-year-old, containing exactly the same provisions as the Commons amendment before us, and had been passed without a division, but had failed to proceed for lack of time. He had introduced his bill in order that we could keep properly separate the issues of embryo research and abortion (both of which he feared would be lumped together as falling under the heading 'the protection of the unborn child'). We were now being asked to vote on the same issue; but the stakes were higher. There had also been time for the pro-life groups to marshal their supporters in the House. Lord Houghton himself was furious. He accused the House of Commons of seeking a way out of the problem they had in finding time for private bills by laying open the path for this matter to be spatchcocked into this bill. 'Here it comes', he said, 'as a flaming carbuncle on the body politic of the Human Fertilization and Embryology Bill. Here we are, up against the time-limit of the session.' He was particularly enraged because when his bill had been debated and passed the House was virtually empty. Most of the pro-life and Roman Catholic members were not in their places, because they felt certain that the bill would get nowhere. Only now were they alert, and eager to throw out an amendment that was the same as the bill they had allowed to pass.

A majority of those who spoke that evening were hostile to the abortion amendment. Many said that we must not be moved by the thought of the 'inconvenience' that would be caused if we sent the bill back to the House of Commons. Those who were conscientiously opposed both to abortion and to research using human embryos saw it as their duty to send it back, and tell the Commons to do better. I did not see it as mere 'inconvenience'. We had been told by the Lord Chancellor himself that if we sent the bill back, having rejected the amendment, then as the end of the session was approaching, we would probably lose the whole bill. And I found that I minded about this more than I thought I would.

Though while the committee of inquiry had been sitting I had hoped that our recommendations would be accepted by government, I had not confidently expected it. But as the months, indeed years, had passed, I became more and more committed to the kind of legislation we had proposed. Besides, when I had handed over the report, in 1984, I was in no way concerned with legislation myself. Now I was in a small way part of the process. If we lost the bill at the eleventh hour I should feel that I personally ought to have done more to ensure its passage. Instead, though I had talked to a good many people who I believed would help it through, I had not been particularly energetic about actually speaking up for it in the Chamber. I thought, on this particular evening, that Lord Houghton, much as I admired him, had probably turned people against the bill by his manifest indignation against those who had not taken his private bill seriously. So I expected the Commons amendment to be rejected.

But all was well. After many speeches, a substantial majority voted in favour of that Commons amendment and all the others proposed, and by about ten o'clock in the evening it was all over and the bill was passed. I felt enormous relief, and also incredulity that what I had been working on, on and off, for nearly six years was now no longer any business of mine.

During the early 1990s the provisions of the Act seemed to work well, under the regulation and monitoring of the now statutory Human Fertilization and Embryology Authority, set up with Ruth Deech, a lawyer, and Principal of St Anne's College, Oxford, as its firm and highly intelligent chairman. Meanwhile there was still considerable optimism about developing ways of identifying faulty genes in embryos fertilized in the laboratory. What was or was not to be permissible in this field began to be something that it would fall to the authority to decide, at least for the UK.

In the case of families at risk of having a baby who would suffer from a monogenetic disease such as cystic fibrosis, the couple's eggs and sperm could be fertilized and several embryos produced, and then scrutinized so that only the healthy embryos would be implanted; or, in the case of haemophilia which afflicts only males, only females would be implanted. This was known as pre-implantation selection. This became a generally accepted procedure during this time (though, in contrast with opinion at the time of the passage of the 1990 Act, it was often opposed by members of groups representing people with disabilities. These people had become increasingly hostile to what they saw as an irrational prejudice against their existence. They opposed any measures that would seek to eliminate them, the disabled, from society.) A bolder option was to try actually to remove or replace the faulty gene in either a newly fertilized embryo, or in a child or adult who had been born suffering from the monogenetic disease. This was known as gene therapy.

Opponents of such interventions saw them not as attempts to cure otherwise incurable diseases, but as the beginnings of a full-scale eugenics programme. There were some countries in Europe, especially Germany, where any genetic intervention, whether at the embryonic or a later stage, was outlawed. The history of Nazi eugenics made it impossible for Germans to contemplate any such procedures, though it was not only in Germany that eugenic programmes were carried out in the first half of the twentieth century. More that 60,000 sterilizations for eugenic reasons were carried out in the United States; and involuntary sterilizations of the mentally deficient or those deemed to be morally incompetent were carried out in Norway, Sweden, Switzerland and the Canadian province of Alberta. In some cases such sterilization programmes were still in existence in the 1970s. But, outrageous as they were, they did not shock the world as much as the Nazi attempts to rid the world of Jews.

That those who argued in favour of allowing gene therapy to proceed were seeking to reintroduce eugenics was thus a highly emotionally charged accusation. However, it was very widely agreed, for example in the several conferences set up by the CIBA Foundation (an international scientific and educational charity, funded by the Swiss pharmaceutical company CIBA–Geigy), that while positive eugenics was wrong, genetic manipulation for therapeutic purposes was simply a new extension of beneficent medical interventions to prevent disease. Yet even here there was extreme caution.

In September 1991 a committee under the chairmanship of Sir Cecil Clothier, a lawyer much involved with issues of health, reported to the government, advising that a sharp distinction be drawn between gene therapy practised on somatic cells and that which might be practised on germ cells. Somatic-cell gene therapy would modify or remove a faulty gene in an individual patient who was already suffering from an identified monogenetic disease. It would therefore, if all went well, remove the disease in that individual patient, but have no effects after that patient had died. Germ-cell therapy, on the other hand, would have as its primary aim the prevention of the transmission of defective genes to subsequent generations. This might be brought about by the manipulation of cells containing the faulty genes either in sperm and egg, or in the very early embryo, soon after fertilization, and before the cells had begun to differentiate into those that would form specific parts of the body.

The recommendation of the committee was that, though genetic manipulation of somatic cells, that is cells from a child or an adult, might be permitted, gene modification of the germ-line should not yet be attempted. They concluded that there was simply too much ignorance of what might be the long-term outcome of such manipulation, especially as it might affect the diversity of the human gene-pool, for it to be morally acceptable to embark on germ-cell genetic modification. In paragraph 7.2 of the report, they wrote 'We are clear that there is at present insufficient knowledge to evaluate the risks to future generations of the gene modification of the germ-line.' This distinction and its moral implications became the orthodoxy of the end of the twentieth century, at least in this country and in Europe.

In June 2000 the first draft of the complete map of the human genome was completed (not without a good deal of competitive rancour between the team from Cambridge who were, among others, slowly working on it, and an American team headed by Craig Venter, then chief executive of Celera Genomics, which had discovered short cuts). There are more than 30,000 human genes and their variants. Scientists from all over the world are now busy trying to identify genes that are involved in every possible human condition, not merely the several thousand diseases caused by one faulty gene, but conditions such as obesity, schizophrenia, homosexuality and alcoholism, where more genes than one are involved. But there is still caution about germ-line intervention to remedy genetic defects. In the United States, where there is no government regulation that covers all research in these fields, though federal funding can be withheld from research in the public sector if it is believed to be wrong, there is a head-on clash between people like Eric Lander, head of the Whitehead–MIT Center for Genomic Research (one of the largest sequencing centres for the human genome project in the United States) and Gregory Stock, Director of Medicine Technology and Society at UCLA. Lander said, 'This is the big one: the question whether it's right to modify the genetic code so that people pass on particular traits to their children. For now, I'd like to see a ban on modifying the human germ-line.' On this, Stock, in his recent book, *Redesigning Humans*,* comments: 'Lander's caution is understandable, but it won't have any impact on the end result.' And he goes on to say, 'Two assumptions are implicit in the idea that one day we will be able to purposefully manipulate our genes. First, genes matter and are responsible for important aspects of who we are. Second, many of the influences our genes exert are straightforward enough to identify and select or rework.' And he argues that now that people increasingly make these assumptions, they will simply demand germ-line intervention, either on eggs and sperm or on newly conceived embryos. The market will dictate what happens. It is perhaps worth contrasting Stock's brash economic determinism with the measured remarks of Sir Cecil Clothier at the beginning of the report already mentioned. There he wrote:

> ... significant development in science or technology
> has been accompanied by dangers both known and
> unknown. Society watches this progress with mingled
> admiration and anxiety, the more acute perhaps as
> science gets ever closer to the fundamental controls
> over the nature and composition of living things. To
> prohibit the progress of science in any particular
> direction may well be tyranny; to seek to shape its
> course is surely sensible. In doing so we should be
> careful also to preserve the right of society to
> determine how the achievements of science are used.

---

* Gregory Stock, *Redesigning Humans* (London: Profile Books, 2002).

These are admirable words; and they certainly reflect the frame of mind in which we set about formulating regulations for the use of the new techniques in the 1980s. But are they realistic? The more international and industry-driven research becomes, the less sensible it seems to try to lay down restrictions which, if they can be effective at all, can be so only in one country, and within the compass of one legislature. In the face of the facts of globalization, and the powerful incentive of capturing world markets, efforts to regulate and control advances in technology may seem not just futile but pitiful. Resounding moral principles about preserving the dignity of human beings or even the integrity of the human gene-pool seem to come down to nothing but a bleat: 'Not in my back yard'.

In 1997 perhaps the greatest, and certainly the most widely publicized event in the development of genetic engineering occurred: the birth of Dolly, at the Roslin Institute outside Edinburgh. Dolly was the first mammal to be born as the result not of the fertilization of an egg by semen, but by cell nuclear replacement. An egg was taken from a Scottish Blackface ewe, and its nucleus was extracted, leaving only the very fragile outer shell of the egg (with a few, but important genes still remaining in the mitochondrial cells on the inside of the shell). Into this fragile shell were inserted some mammalian cells taken from another adult ewe, a Finn Dorset, and cultured in the laboratory. An electric current was passed through the egg which made it fuse to form an embryo. This newly constructed embryo was then inserted into the uterus of a third ewe, who became successfully pregnant, acting as a surrogate mother who carried the foetus to term. The whole procedure was both complex and extremely precarious. In the months of experimentation, 277 reconstructed embryos were made, of which only 29 appeared to be in good condition. Thirteen surrogate ewes received these embryos, and in the end only one viable lamb was born. The rest of the embryos aborted at various stages of their development, or were born with gross birth defects. Dolly herself, the one remaining lamb, was rather large, but otherwise perfect, though after five years she is showing signs of premature ageing.

Despite this less than optimistic story, people inevitably began at once to raise the question of whether other animals, including human beings, might not soon be cloned. There have been numerous other mammals cloned since 1997, for various experimental purposes, and doubtless the difficulties of the procedure will be overcome or at least diminished with practice and further research. But this does not answer the question whether at some time in the future human beings might be cloned. There are few possibilities that give rise to such immediate cries of moral outrage as this.

Manifestly, at present the extreme hazard of cloning is itself a moral argument against attempting it in human subjects. No woman, even if she volunteered to act as a subject should be asked to undergo such risks; and if a child were born without obvious defects it still would not be clear what the future of that child might be. Many people, including many doctors, believe that human cloning should never take place, because it will always be impossible to know that it would be safe, however routine in might have become using other animals.

There are many others, however, who believe that, even if the process of cloning became virtually risk-free, it would be morally wrong to carry it out on human beings. What causes this sense of moral outrage cannot be the simple fact that there would be two people in existence with (almost) the same genes (almost, because the mitochondrial genes would be present only in the cloned child, passed down from the donor of the denucleated egg). No one is morally offended by the existence of identical twins, formed naturally by the splitting of the embryo before fourteen days from fertilization; and such twins have completely identical genes. No one says of them, as they do of putative clones, that they are deprived of their most precious right, that of personal identity. Everyone knows that such twins are two different people, separate organisms, physiologically and psychologically. Even Siamese twins are thought of as two people, not one.

Nor does there seem to me to be anything morally objectionable in the fact that these clones would be identical twins separated by a generation, identical father and son. Some argue that it would be appalling for a child to look at his father and see exactly what he would be like when he was the age of his father. But it is doubtful whether this would be especially burdensome. In some respects, of course, it happens already, when there is a strong genetic likeness between father and son. But on the other hand two people, whatever their genes, who are brought up at different times and in a different environment, will have a different education and culture, and will therefore differ in many important ways. They may both go bald early, or both have perfect pitch, but they will have different tunes running in their heads. We are the products of nurture as well as nature.

Another argument has been that everyone has a natural right to be born through sexual intercourse between a man and a woman, and to be born asexually would be an infringement of this right. Of course it is true that everyone in the world is now, and has always been, born as a result of sexual reproduction, even if the egg and sperm were joined together in the laboratory; but I find it difficult to understand what would be meant by saying that to be born thus constitutes a right.

For my part, I can imagine that, if and only if the procedure were safe, there might be an argument for using cloning in certain cases of otherwise irremediable infertility, for couples who desperately wanted a child. For I believe that the revulsion that is felt towards the thought of making human clones in fact arises out of social and political fears, fears, that is to say, of where it might lead if it came to be widely practised. Visions of power-crazed dictators are invoked, who would cause cloned armies to be created, or armies of people so docile and unambitious that they would contentedly work in nasty jobs for low pay. For the more we know of the human genome, the more we fear that not merely genes expressed in diseases will be identified, but those expressed in all kinds of intellectual and personality traits as well; and we already know that genes can be changed in animal clones, introduced or eliminated at the stage of transferring cells into the denucleated egg. So in theory an unending succession of human clones could be produced, with whatever characteristics were chosen. Such fears of a Brave New World should not have any relevance, if human cloning were limited by law to the remedying of certain specific malfunctions. But I recognize that such a view will never prevail, not only because, as I have said, it is highly probable that human cloning will never be sufficiently risk-free for it to be tried, but also because this is the kind of area within which the slippery slope argument has the greatest hold over the mind.

If once a human baby is cloned, it will be argued, no matter within what legal or regulative restriction, other human clones will follow, and the human species will have embarked on an inevitable slide down the slope to a world

where people can be made to order, according to the prevailing view of political, social or medical correctness. We
must never put our foot on the slope, or we will not be able
to halt the descent. It is a powerful image, and it speaks to a
deep fear of being manipulated, of our becoming helpless
pawns in someone else's game.

We have somehow, during the twentieth century, collec-
tively lost our nerve. We expect that political power, calling
on science and technology will be used for ill rather than
good. This is why Huxley's *Brave New World* and Orwell's
*Nineteen Eighty-Four* have proved such compelling myths.
And the history of the century is undoubtedly enough to
explain our timidity. Scientists, even more than politicians,
are seen as the sole inheritors of Victorian confidence in
beneficent progress along the technological road, which is in
fact the road to ruin. They are not to be trusted. Neither
faith nor hope is a fashionable virtue.

Yet, though politicians have to pay attention to popular
fears, they are also anxious that their country shall not fall
behind in the profitable race down the dread technological
road. They are torn; and this conflict of interests is well
illustrated by the legislation introduced in the years 2001
and 2002, both in this country and in the United States.
Since the birth of Dolly, there has been an extraordinary
explosion of research and discovery in the field of genetics
and biotechnology, and legislation limps behind technology.

In June 2000 a virtually complete map of the human
genome was published, the result, as I have said, of an uneasy
coalition between a respectable genetics institute in Cambridge and a rather more suspect commercial firm, Celera
Genomics, in the United States, headed at the time by Craig
Ventner. (In spite of the general agreement that samples
used to make the map of the human genome must be taken

from a wide range of people and strictly anonymized, it later emerged that he had used his own tissue for much of the work of his company).

As more has been learned about the way cells, and genes within cells, function, so new medical advances have begun to seem possible. In particular, research on human stem cells has emerged as a potentially fruitful source of therapy for conditions at present untreatable, such as Parkinson's disease and Alzheimer's, as well as for severe burns or massive spinal-cord injury. Stem cells, which occur in all human tissue at all stages of development, are cells capable of dividing, so that one of the two 'daughter' cells retains the characteristics of the stem cell, the other differentiates into a specific type of cell, such as a neural cell or a blood cell. In this way the cells of the whole body are renewed. But in adult human tissue it is difficult to identify which cells are stem cells, and the capability of such cells, if isolated, to differentiate over a wide range of types of cell is thought to be limited.

However, in the very early embryo, at what is called the blastocyst stage, reached after about five days of embryonic development, none of the 50 to 100 cells has differentiated: all are totipotent, that is, they may develop into any of the 200 or so cells that make up the human body. The ultimate aim of stem-cell research is, by the use of these embryonic stem cells, to build up 'banks' of cells of particular types, which will renew themselves for ever, so that if, for example, the cells of someone's liver have failed, instead of a whole liver transplant, he might receive a liver-cell transplant, and the new cell would regenerate the whole liver, and go on regenerating it indefinitely.

Cell transplant could be used in any organ, including organs such as the brain which cannot be treated by organ transplant (in spite of the science-fictional examples of brain transplants, beloved of some philosophers exploring the subject of personal identity). The first step in such research must be to extract stem cells from early embryos, and cause them to differentiate into specific cells to start to build up the banks. Once these banks are established, there will be no further need for the use of embryos; but at present they constitute an essential research tool.

The Human Fertilization and Embryology Act (1990) had permitted the use of human embryos for research, under licence, up to fourteen days from fertilization, but only for certain prescribed purposes, namely for research into issues of fertility or infertility, or contraception. But it had been left open for regulations to be brought in to change these restrictions, should it in future be thought necessary to do so. By 1998 pressure was building up on the government, both from universities and from pharmaceutical companies, as well as from research bodies such as the Medical Research Council, to widen the scope of the 1990 Act, so that licences might be sought for research using early embryos to include research into the use of embryonic stem cells, and the mechanisms of differentiation, ultimately for therapeutic purposes that had nothing to do with fertility. Accordingly, in September 1999 a committee was set up under the chairmanship of the Chief Medical Officer, Sir Liam Donaldson, to examine the benefits that might come from embryonic stem-cell research, and to determine whether the scope of research under the 1990 Act should be widened. The committee recommended that such regulations should be brought in, and these regulations were debated and passed in the House of Commons in December 2000, and came to be debated in the House of Lords in January 2001. Here government was manifestly swayed by the arguments of scientists and industrialists, and inclined to overlook the fears of the public.

But, understandably, the pro-life group saw this as a chance to reopen the whole question of whether it was morally tolerable that early embryos should be used for research at all. Their leader in the House of Lords was Lord Alton, who had been a consistent opponent of embryo research, both when he was in the House of Commons, and after he became a peer. Though I had no sympathy with their moral scruples about research, I had some sympathy with their strong feeling that these new regulations were being rushed through, without proper time for those who opposed them to put their case. They had felt, without justification I think, that in 1990 they had somehow been cheated of their opportunity to make their case against embryo research, and now here they were again, with little opportunity for a full-scale discussion of what was still the fundamental issue, namely whether it was morally permissible to use early embryos for research and then destroy them.

There were numerous peripheral arguments deployed against the new regulations. One was that adult stem cells would be just as good for the purposes of research as embryonic stem cells. But most of the scientific evidence was that, as I have said, adult stem cells are both more difficult to isolate, and less capable of differentiating into other types of cell than embryonic stem cells.

The other argument that not unexpectedly was given a great deal of support was the 'slippery slope' argument. The process of producing embryos by nuclear cell transfer and then using the stem cells of these embryos for therapeutic purpose had together come to be known as 'therapeutic cloning' (as opposed to 'reproductive cloning', which would involve the transfer of the newly reconstituted embryo into a uterus and the birth of a whole animal). This was an unfortunate name. That the process of making the new embryo was the same as that used in the cloning of Dolly was in fact irrelevant, because the whole process would have been futile if the embryo had been allowed to develop beyond the blastocyst stage, when its cells were totipotent. Moreover, it was doubly irrelevant, because most of the early embryos to be use in stem-cell research would be 'spare' embryos, left over from IVF treatments, where fertilized embryos tended to be too numerous for implantation, and therefore destined to be destroyed anyway. The whole issue of stem-cell research had really nothing whatever to do with the question of the cloning of whole human beings. But the slippery slope argument was brought out time and again.

At the end of many hours of debate in the House of Lords, Lord Walton of Detchant proposed a soothing, though manifestly pointless, amendment to bring it about that if these regulations were permitted there should be a select committee of the House of Lords to examine all the scientific and ethical issues surrounding embryonic stem-cell research, and if this committee when it reported so recommended the regulations would be considered again. Everyone, whichever side they were on, realized that if the regulations were once allowed they would not be revoked whatever the select committee reported. But for the time being it seemed a kind of concession; and the regulations were duly agreed to in the House of Lords as they had been in the House of Commons. In fact the select committee, which reported in February 2002, and had worked very hard under the chairmanship of the Bishop of Oxford, Richard Harries, did an excellent job, and their report is a useful place to find all the facts then known about embryonic stem-cell research. They found, as expected, in favour of the research being allowed to proceed, and the report was formally accepted.

Meanwhile, in November 2001, one of the pro-life groups made an attempt to show that the 1990 Act, which had made the cloning of human embryos a criminal offence, would not cover the case of embryos created by cell nuclear replacement, and thus cloning using such embryos was not ruled out. It had been assumed up to then that all human cloning was covered. But on 15 November Mr Justice Crane ruled that embryos created by cell nuclear replacement were not covered, since in the relevant part of the Act the words are that clones may not be made from embryos 'once fertilization is complete'. In 1989, when the law was drafted, it was not thought possible to produce a whole embryo by cell nuclear replacement; the only known method, though it had never been used, was that of dividing the cells of the very early embryo, before differentiation of the cells, so that each portion would have the same genetic material. This would be reproducing artificially the way that identical twins are formed naturally. We, in our 1984 report, in fact made no recommendation about cloning, but merely noticed that this would be one possible future development. The law, however, contained a specific prohibition, and the drafters presumably took it for granted that the prohibition would apply to any embryo. They need not in fact have added the words 'once fertilization is complete'; they were strictly redundant, since fertilization was the only way then that an embryo could be produced. Mr Justice Crane, however, was bound to follow the actual words; and he understood them to exclude from the prohibition embryos produced otherwise than by fertilization. Indeed he ruled, rather oddly, that embryos produced by cell nuclear fission were not strictly

139

speaking embryos. This entailed, as the pro-lifers had hoped, that under the 1990 Act cloning by cell nuclear transfer was not prohibited; and they were sure that once this was understood, people would rush ahead with human cloning (of which naturally they totally disapproved). They were partly vindicated, indeed, because immediately the loophole in the UK law became known, a notoriously excitable Italian, Professor Antinori, announced that he was coming to England, where he had an English colleague, and 200 women who had volunteered their services as surrogates, and he would have cloned a human baby within a year.

This announcement produced panic in the government, who instantly produced a bill to make placing an embryo produced by cell nuclear transfer in a woman's uterus a criminal offence. The bill was rushed through both Houses of Parliament with extraordinary speed, and Professor Antinori was frustrated. Many of us thought the legislation unnecessary. In the UK, he could not have carried out his research without a licence, and the Human Fertilization and Embryology Authority had already made it clear that they would never issue a licence for research aimed at human cloning. But here the government listened to the timid among the public, rather than to scientists. At least, with legislation in place, the slippery slope has been blocked, as far as this country is concerned. No human cloning may be tried.

In the United States politicians have shown even more uncertainty and prevarication. For a long time there was no federal funding of IVF, or of any research using live embryos. But of course research and treatment proceeded unregulated in private laboratories and clinics. The market led. After the birth of Dolly, a moratorium was called on all cloning by cell nuclear replacement, but this was soon called off, and a good deal of work has been done on the cloning of animals. When the question of stem-cell research arose, first President Bush insisted that it should be banned, and no embryos should be used, whether produced by fertilization or otherwise. Here he was succumbing to the arguments of the pro-life lobby. Then he proposed, presumably under pressure from science and industry, who argued that the United States would fall far behind in the biotechnology race if no cell-lines could be used or cell-banks established, that the few cell-lines that had already been isolated could be used, but no new ones created. This of course was an absurd position to adopt, especially as most of the cell-lines that were likely to be useful, either for increasing knowledge of the mechanisms of differentiation or for the development of specific drugs, had already been patented and were not accessible. In any case, if it was supposed to be wrong to use embryos for this kind of work, and then destroy them, surely it should not make any difference whether they had been destroyed before or after a particular date. Maybe he thought that at least his hands would be clean. At any rate, US scientists who want to work in the field of therapeutic cloning or stem-cell research are temporarily in a confusing and inhibiting position, and many of them are taking their work elsewhere.

But these conflicting voices, and regulations that differ in different countries, inevitably raise questions within the pharmaceutical industries, both in their own research and development departments, and in any partnership between industry and the universities. The work can be taken anywhere in the world. There are those in the United States, such as Professor Gregory Stock from UCLA, who argue that to attempt regulation is futile. In his book *Redesigning Humans,* he suggests that we should stop worrying, and let the market dictate what is to be done. If people want their babies to be fitted out with genes to make them healthier, taller, cleverer than they would otherwise be, then scientists will provide what they want, and they will pay up. Whatever turns out to be possible will be wanted, and we should leave it for our children and grandchildren to adapt to the resulting changed society. Reading this kind of book makes one feel ridiculous for fussing so much about licensing research, or the moral evils of cloning human beings. And it seems especially small-minded when one reflects that the most one can do is prevent the things one does not like in the small confines of one's own backyard. In fact, the latest advances in biotechnology are more likely to come from China than from anywhere else; and we have no way of controlling what those advances will be, or how they will be used.

Yet I must confess to the feeling that I, at least, am not quite ready for total *laissez-faire*. There is something to be said for trying to achieve some kind of moral consensus about what is tolerable and what is not, when we contemplate the new technologies which inevitably seem sometimes dangerous and socially unpredictable in their long-term consequences. I am still, on the whole, of the opinion, as I was in 1984, that regulation is better than prohibition, and that if one country seems to be getting it about right, others may follow. But I have also to admit that to say this makes more sense when one is thinking about Europe, even about Europe and the United States, than when one starts to think about the great technological advances coming from the Far East, where there is so hugely different a culture.

There have been other consequences of the revolution in genetics, many of them problems still unresolved. The most recalcitrant of these concern the ownership of genetic information. I became unexpectedly involved in an acute

142

example of such a problem in December 1998, when I was rung up by a barely intelligible and quite unknown person from the University of Reykjavik and asked if I would go over the next week to talk at a conference about confidentiality in the setting up of a genetic databank. I was involved in a small-scale problem of the kind as a member of the ethical advisory committee to Marks & Spencer, who have a valuable data bank of genetic data from all their women staff, which goes back over many years, and was set up as a joint venture between the company and the British Heart Foundation, as part of a research project on women's coronary health in relation to job and diet. Now other companies were asking whether they might make use of this material. The blood specimens had been taken with the consent of the women involved, but only for the specific use of which they had been told. There was about to be a new problem as to whether they should be asked for more open-ended consent, and who, if anyone, owned the blood samples. So I thought I knew a little about the kind of things I should say at the conference, and I looked forward to getting a wider view of the issues involved. Besides, I had never been to Iceland, and I looked forward to that as well. So I wrote an anodyne little piece, and set off the next week.

I arrived just in time for an evening party to launch the conference, which was to start the following morning. The party was held in the University, and I met not only the man to whom I had talked on the telephone (he was the only one whose English was not impeccable) but most of the Department of Biochemistry, who were young and enthusiastic, and all had doctorates from either Harvard or Cambridge, having done their first degrees at home.

There was an air of extreme agitation in the room, with people gathering in little knots and exclaiming, and others rushing out of the room apparently to listen to the radio news. Someone said to me, 'Stefansson is coming to the first session of the conference. Luckily he's not here tonight.' I had no idea who Stefansson was, nor why his presence would have been controversial; and at last, when the official guests had left, I managed to sit down with my hosts, while they told me what had happened.

Kari Stefansson, who had been educated partly at the University of Chicago and had spent fifteen years in the Department of Medicine there, before becoming a professor of neurology at Harvard, had come back to Iceland a few years before and set up a company on the outskirts of Reykjavik. This company, called Decode, was to hold a huge bank of genetic samples from Icelanders. The deal was that in exchange for money from pharmaceutical companies, especially the Swiss-based company Hoffmann la Roche, Decode would undertake to discover the genes responsible for major diseases, and give the companies exclusive rights to the information, the use of which would enable them to develop and patent drugs. The deal with Roche allowed Decode to equip itself with immensely sophisticated gene-sequencing equipment, and all the computers needed for the work. Stefansson, the managing director, also needed access to the medical records of the entire Icelandic population, and the assurance that the medical profession would cooperate, by taking blood samples from all their patients, with their consent. Roche had undertaken that if this information was made available, it would in exchange supply any drugs developed free to all of Iceland. To legalize this deal, primary legislation would be necessary.

Medical care in Iceland is extremely efficient, and medical records are kept on everyone from birth to death. Moreover, people in Iceland are almost obsessive about keeping their own family records. Their names, both male and female, are all patronymics; and because the population is so small, and because there has been so little immigration over the centuries, there is a complex and well-documented network of family relationships. This is a central part of Icelandic culture. Almost the only cultural heritage the country possesses is the body of Icelandic Sagas, all of which start with an elaborate list of the family connections of the protagonists. Putting all these records into the computers at the same time as isolating the genes in the samples would give Decode a uniquely coherent set of data.

The realization that this was so, and that it would be of enormous value to pharmaceutical companies, was what had brought Stefansson back from the United States to set up Decode. He had persuaded the government to introduce a bill to legalize his contract in the spring of 1998. After that a period of consultation was promised. But on December 17 1998, the very day that I arrived in Rekjiavik, parliament had passed the bill by a majority of seventeen (37 to 20, with six abstentions). It was the last day of the session, and parliament had dissolved before the news broke.

The scientists in the university were appalled. They were no longer worried about how to protect the confidentiality of medical records; they were entirely concerned with the fact that they would no longer have access to the records or the tissue samples. They would have no chance either to carry out their own fundamental research, nor to establish their own contracts with industrial companies. Such contracts had until now been an important means of financing the university and funding research fellowships. I realized that my little talk about confidentiality would be hopelessly out of place at this critical moment. So I went back to my hotel and wrote a quite different paper about academic freedom, and the dangers of commercial interests being allowed to strangle fundamental research. I was well aware that this sort of controversy was familiar enough in the UK. At Girton, for example, we had a Glaxo research fellowship, funded by the company, and one of the conditions attached to the funding was that Glaxo should have first sight of any results the fellow wished to publish. This was hard, even if Glaxo decided they could not use the work, because it entailed a long delay before publication, just when the holder of the fellowship was likely to be seeking a new job, and a good list of publications would be crucial. But I was also aware that it was becoming increasingly difficult to draw a clear line between fundamental and applied research (and this blurring of the line is still more manifest now than it was in 1998), and that, in medicine especially, research was unlikely to be funded unless it could be shown to have useful application.

At any rate I scrambled together a rather sketchy paper, and went to bed just before 5 a.m. The conference began at 9 a.m., and there at the back of the lecture room I saw one of the most enormous men I had ever set eyes on. Like almost the entire Icelandic population, he had piercing blue eyes and fair hair, in his case turning grey. It was impossible not to see him in a Viking's helmet, striding the Wagnerian stage. No one had to point him out to me: I knew at once that he was Stefansson. After various formalities, I read my paper. When it was done, my new friends from the Department of Microbiology were pleased and congratulatory, but Stefansson seemed very angry. He stalked out.

The conference was less than informative for me. I had been told that all the papers would either be given in English or would be simultaneously translated from Icelandic. As it turned out, all the papers except mine and that of one Belgian contributer were in Icelandic, and the translating apparatus had broken down. So I spent a good deal of time walking round the city (which I loved), and being taken out into the country by my new friends. The talk was almost all about the rights of Decode against those of the University; and there was a plan to get GPs and medical centres to refuse to cooperate in the deal. After I went home, the rows became increasingly bitter, both between the scientists, the government and Decode, and also between Hoffmann la Roche and other pharmaceutical companies. And many people in Iceland felt that they had been exploited for wholly commercial purposes. No one was better aware than they that their genetic data was a unique treasure. They felt that they owned this treasure, and that what wealth was to be derived from it should be theirs. After all, the promise of free drugs was not much of a reward, especially as to develop a new drug, put it through all its trials and market it takes many years. I do not know what the state of popular and scientific feeling is now. But I believe that things have settled down, as the prospects for local employment in Decode have greatly improved an economy hitherto largely dependent on fish.

I have told this saga in order to illustrate the complex problems, moral and legal, that follow the new biotechnology. What has happened in the last twenty years or so constitutes a scientific revolution as great as the discovery of the circulation of the blood. And in my view, it causes us to rethink our position in the world as urgently as we had to in the days of Galileo. Then, we had to get used to the idea that the earth was not central to the universe, but was a planet among many. Now, we may have to get used to the thought that we share our genes not only with other animals, but even with plants. Since Darwin, we have recognized that we are more closely embedded in the natural world than theology and the Age of Reason had placed us; now we may have to accept a further fact. Just as, being a bright and successful species, we have always manipulated the rest of nature for our own ends, we are now beginning to be able to manipulate ourselves. Starting on my Greats course in Oxford in 1946, the first philosophy text I read was a book by the Cambridge philosopher C. D. Broad, called *The Mind and its Place in Nature*. Perhaps it is time that someone purloined that title. In the following chapter, I want to look at one aspect of the question of how to define the place of the mind of man, by considering our relation with animals with lesser minds than our own.

# 4 Man and Other Animals

Since the mid-nineteenth century we have lived through what amounts to a biological revolution that has affected everyone's thinking, not merely that of scientists. This revolution, as I have said, has been as great as that of Copernicus, forcing us to think of our place in nature in a wholly new way. We cannot (or those of us who are not deliberately dogmatic and anti-rational cannot) go back to a pre-Darwinian world, or a world before the evidence of geology, and what it told us about the slow beginnings of life on earth, gradually came to light. We cannot accept a history in which human beings were created in God's image on the sixth day, and were given dominion over the earth and all the other creatures on it. And so, the old articles of faith having been taken away, the question has urgently arisen of how we ought to behave towards the natural world, of which we are so much more a part than it had seemed before. How should we value animals other than ourselves? And, depending on the answer to that question, to what extent is it morally right that we should use them for our own purposes? Are human beings justified in treating themselves as a race apart? For there is no doubt that this is what most of us unthinkingly do. Even if, on conscientious grounds, some people become vegetarians and so do not eat animals, still most of them are not averse to clothing themselves in their wool or skins, riding them, racing them or keeping them as pets. This is to use other animals in a way that we would not contemplate using humans. Endless books have been written, especially in the last twenty years, about what ought to be our attitude to the natural world, and especially to animals. Now that we know that humans have very few genes that are peculiarly human, most being shared not only with the great apes, but with mice, fruit-flies and even plants, ought we not radically to revise the traditional view of human dominion over the world, or even stewardship of it? Should we not take the sufferings of animals exactly as seriously as we take those of our fellow humans? Should we not even accord them rights? To do otherwise has been termed 'speciesism', as supposedly prejudiced and indefensible as sexism and racism.

As has been usual in my life, I found such questions philosophically interesting, and was long prepared to set undergraduate essays on them, and discuss them in tutorials. But then, suddenly, in the late 1970s, I had to try to think about the use of animals in a less abstract way, when I was invited to join a Home Office committee set up, at first, to consider a form of toxicity-testing called the LD 50 test. I really had no idea at all what I had got into; and I still retain very little memory of this committee, except that it was chaired by a somewhat distant but amiable character called Lord Cross. (I had agreed to join the committee under the mistaken belief that the chairman was someone I knew, another Lord Cross, multiply married, one of whose daughters, Venetia, had been a pupil at the Oxford High School when I was headmistress, a girl I greatly liked, but who was not very confident.)

The LD 50 test was coming under increasing fire from people interested in animal welfare (as well as those interested in animal rights). Before putting a drug on the market, pharmaceutical companies are required by law to subject the drug to tests using animals, and then tests using human volunteers, and finally to clinical tests, using patients suffering from the condition the drug is supposed to remedy. In the 1970s the animal test required was the amazingly crude and wasteful LD 50 test, a short-term test to rule out acute toxicity. It was first designed to assess the potency of known toxins such as digitalis, which might nevertheless be used for therapy in low doses. Later, it came to be used as a more general safety test. The object of the test was to evaluate the single dose required to kill 50 per cent of the animals treated, over a specified time. The original tests used 60–80 animals, with no upper limit to the doses permitted. This involved the often painful death of a high proportion of animals in the test group.

The crudity of this test was obvious. After all, almost any substance is poisonous if absorbed in high enough quantities, and it was left to those who administered the test to determine how high a dose should be given to the animals, in the test of any substance. We recommended that a different test of toxicity should be used, the 'fixed-dose procedure' (FDP) which used only ten animals for each substance to be tested. Each animal was given a predetermined dose (the amount based on the known properties of the substance) and killed either at the end of the test (probably fourteen days) or as soon as the first signs of poisoning became apparent. Thus a great deal of animal suffering would be eliminated. By 1991, the LD50 test had been dropped by the First International Conference on Harmonization of European Law as a requirement for the sale of medicines, and the FDP put in its place. Since the year 2000 the Home Office in the UK has not, routinely, issued any licence for toxicity-testing that involves the LD50.

The Home Office Advisory Committee on Animal Experiments, being a committee of the Home Office, was not obliged to raise the fundamental question of whether it was morally acceptable to use animals at all in toxicity-testing. Indeed few fundamental questions of any kind were raised. The whole institutional ethos of the Home Office, with its team of inspectors, was based on the assumption that animals might be used, but their use subjected to scrutiny. The question before the committee was whether it was morally tolerable that animals (nearly always rats and mice) should be subjected to tests that involved waiting to die, in more or less painful circumstances, and where there was so much laxity in the amount of the dosage to be given to each animal. These questions were, of course, disguised questions about the morality of the use of other animals, for strictly human ends, especially when, in the nature of the case, the animals used would suffer pain and premature death. But the disguise remained. The framework within which the committee deliberated was that the use of animals for research was essential, but that it must be regulated and supervised. But if there was to be regulation on moral grounds, which was the presumption of the committee, and of the Home Office under whose aegis we had been called into existence, according to what criteria of acceptability was this regulation to be established? This was the question before us.

As usual at the beginning of work on a committee of this kind, I found myself floundering in my own ignorance of the facts, and in the limitations of our terms of reference. In those days (I think it is better now) no one gave one much of a briefing before one's first meeting, or if there was a briefing, it came in the form of somewhat technical papers, and one had little chance to raise idiot questions. Apart from one representative of the RSPCA, there was no one on the committee to question what the inspectors and others acquainted with laboratory animals told us about what was a tolerable degree of pain or stress that an animal might suffer in experimental treatment. Moreover, I soon became aware of a considerable defensiveness on the part of the Home Office, anxious to preserve what had always been done as the blueprint for the future. So I sat rather quietly, taking little part in the discussion, and before I had really learned enough to feel confident to speak, the recommendations were drawn up, and in early 1979 we advised ministers that the LD50 test should be dropped as a routine requirement for the testing of drugs.

I thought, with some relief, that my days at the Home Office were over. But before I knew where I was, Lord Cross told me that he was retiring, and that the committee would now have a new remit, and that I would be its chairman. I had never felt so ill-prepared for any task. But by the early part of 1980 the committee had been restructured, renamed (we were now the Home Office Advisory Committee on Animal Experiments) and we had been given our terms of reference, which included 'to consider ... proposals for revision of the law'. Until this time, the regulation of laboratory research using live animals had been carried out under the Cruelty to Animals Act of 1876, an act that had been passed originally with the intention of criminalizing the cruel treatment of animals in streets and other open places, and in particular of offering protection to horses against their ill-usage by cabbies. (Anna Sewell's tear-jerker *Black Beauty* had been part of the campaign for legislation.) It was certainly high time that a bill was introduced that would

properly address the wholly new circumstances of laboratory research. The word 'cruelty' in the title of the 1876 Act
made it wholly unsuitable as the vehicle of licensing the use
of animals: no one would seriously suggest that cruelty
should in some circumstances be licensed. And the retention
of the word 'cruelty' played into the hands of the antivivisectionists, who were already clamouring for a complete
prohibition on animal experimentation.

In the early part of 1979 a bill had been introduced in the
House of Lords entitled The Laboratory Animals Protection
Bill. On 25 October that year, the bill received its second
reading, and at the end of the debate it was sent for examination to a select committee, whose report and amendments
to the bill were published in April 1980. This select committee had met on about sixteen occasions, and had taken
oral evidence, as well as receiving written evidence from a
number of bodies. They presented an amended bill to the
House of Lords in April, but still it was not accepted. Instead
our Home Office committee was charged with the task of
examining the bill, as amended by the select committee, and
reporting to the Minister. The outcome of our deliberations
was published in 1981, and legislation was finally passed in
1986. It had been a long process.

All the time that we were scrutinizing the bill, we knew more
or less what we were doing. With the help of the Home
Office Inspectorate, and other Home Office civil servants, we
had to decide whether the new bill, if it became law, would
actually work. There was a danger that the whole process of
applying for a licence, both for the individual scientist who
wished to use animals, and for the laboratory at which they
would be kept for use, as well as for the specific research
project for which he wished to use them, would be too

cumbersome. Throughout our deliberations we were acutely aware that though most members of the public wanted the reassurance that drugs had been tested on animals, and most were in favour of the proposition that research into diseases and possible cures should be carried out using animals, many (and many of the same people) increasingly felt that animals must not be subjected to any pain at all in the course of research, not even the momentary pain of an injection to render them unconscious for the duration of the experiment. Our aim in imposing the restrictions on research, and in demanding scrutiny by the inspectorate of all applications for licences, and of all premises where animals were used, whether for routine mandatory toxicity-testing or for research, was to give the public the reassurance they were increasingly coming to need that no 'cruelty' would be involved at any point. Only responsible people would be permitted to use animals; and the animals would be anaesthetized during any procedure, and, in most cases, killed when the experiment was over, so that they could not suffer any long-term damage.

The more we sought to ensure that no one could get away with a frivolous or unnecessary use of animals, and the more we tried to lay down regulations to ensure that an animal that was suffering irreversible damage should be destroyed immediately, even if the experiment was not completed, the more of a bureaucratic tangle we created. Those members of the committee who were themselves laboratory animal-users recognized that this was so, and sought to simplify the proposed licensing procedures. Those of us who were not professionally involved, on the other hand, thought that nothing less than what we proposed would serve to reassure the public. We simply assumed that the more difficult it was to get a licence, and the more probing the questions to be answered about each procedure to be carried out, the better the life of laboratory animals would become. I now think this was a mistaken belief.

However, it was an agreeable enough committee, and we worked very hard at this stage of our existence. One member whom I met for the first time was Richard Adrian, Master of Pembroke College Cambridge, and the son of the first Lord Adrian who had been Master of Trinity. He became a friend, both in Cambridge and at the House of Lords, until his sad early death from cancer. Richard was an extremely nice modest man, and I instantly made him vice-chairman of the committee, on which he was in fact far more influential than I, being a biologist and a one-time licence-holder himself, and having been a member of the House of Lords select committee, which had recently reported.

Another marvellously clever and helpful member of the committee was Gordon Dunstan, still at that time Professor of Moral and Social Theology at King's College, London, having previously been a canon of Windsor. I had first met him in very different circumstances, in 1950. He was then the newly appointed vicar of the village of Sutton Courtney, near Oxford, where my parents-in-law had retired in 1949. He was totally unsuited to the job, being scholarly and, in appearance at least, austere, and extremely intimidating to the villagers. He told me later, when I got to know him properly, that he had been appointed by mistake, his CV having been confused with that of someone else called Dunstan. He was hoping for an academic job, or at least the chaplaincy of an Oxford college. But he took the post offered, feeling that it would be good for him to lead the life of an ordinary clergyman in a large country parish. He suffered greatly, was unpopular, and I think benefited in no way at all. At any rate I wanted our children to be baptized, and Geoffrey went along with this, so when our eldest daughter, Kitty, was a few weeks old we went to see Gordon Dunstan in the vicarage, to ask him to perform the ceremony. He put us though the most terrifying inquisition about our beliefs, shaky in my case and non-existent in Geoffrey's, and our motives for wishing our baby to be baptized. But in the end, reluctantly, he agreed to carry out the task. He also baptized our next child, Felix, but, having done it once, was not so fierce about doing it a second time. He was so unworldly that he proposed to name his own eldest son Gregory Oliver Dunstan, and it was not until my mother-in-law pointed out to him how this boy might suffer from his initials that he changed the order of the names.

When we met again, on the committee, he had for years been thoroughly in his element as a clear-headed moral and theological philosopher, and a much-valued member of ethical advisory committees, looking as austere as ever, but plainly no longer suffering. There was one occasion when an issue arose in our discussions which he and I went off to talk about in his room in King's College, and to report back to the committee (an instance of the commonly held but false belief that philosophers can actually solve moral problems). I am still not certain about the solution to the problem. It was this: when seeking a licence to carry out work using animals, a scientist must undertake that his research cannot be carried out in any other way, and that he will use as small a number of animals as possible. When we were discussing this part of the proposed legislation, I suddenly raised the question of why it mattered that the numbers of animals should be kept low. If a scientifically better result could be obtained by using a lot of animals, what was against it? The obvious and immediate response of the committee was that our intention was to reduce the suffering of animals, and therefore it followed that as few animals as possible must suffer. I argued that in the case of laboratory mice, it did not really make sense to think of the amount of suffering as a kind of aggregate. We must certainly try to ensure that each mouse suffered as little as possible. But since laboratory mice are far from an endangered species, and since the suffering of each mouse would not be increased by the thought of all the other mice who were suffering with him, nor by a sense of injustice that mice were being wantonly sacrificed for ends that they had not chosen, as would be the case if humans were being used experimentally, I could not see that numbers really mattered. Gordon Dunstan was inclined to agree with me, and we sat one sunny morning in his room discussing the issue, and comparing the death of human beings with the death of animals, and the difference between the horror of mass slaughter and the horror of an individual death. It was the best kind of conversation, wide-ranging, but undertaken with a view to reaching a conclusion of some sort. In the end we agreed to leaving in the clause about using as few animals as possible in each experiment, but only because it would reassure people that animals were not to be frivolously used, not because we thought that in fact the suffering of twenty mice was worse than the suffering of one. I still think that the Home Office figures, which they must by law publish every year, about the numbers of animals used are virtually meaningless; it is of far more interest to those who wish to protect animals to know how many of the animals used really suffered, but the Home Office categories of severity are not particularly informative on this point, as they themselves are now inclined to admit.

After I finally managed to extricate myself from the Home Office committee, which was not until 1985, I met Gordon

Dunstan again in extraordinary circumstances. In 1990, the King of Morocco decided to set up a conference in Agadir to discuss the new legislation in the UK regulating assisted conception. I was invited to explain to the assembled Arabs the thinking that lay behind the law, and Gordon Dunstan was invited to represent the Christian faith. He had been instructed by the Foreign Office, through whom these invitations came, that he must bring his full canonical dress. The conference was held in a huge and hideous hotel, miles from the sea, and half of the hotel was full of enormous Germans, who sat all day by the swimming pool, topless, turning scarlet in the sun – a really incredibly unappealing sight even to non-Muslims. The rest of the hotel was full of pious Muslims, from all over the Arab countries, all men, who had assembled to hear about IVF.

I had to speak first, and I mumbled through the usual explanations and justifications for IVF, research using pre-fourteen-day embryos, and so on. This was followed by speech after speech about the corruption of the West, the demise of morality, the insidious lowering of standards of behaviour, the condoning of murder, the shamelessness of women, the absence of religion. It was agony, all the worse because these remarks were addressed exclusively to me, the only Westerner to have spoken, indeed the only one present except for Gordon Dunstan and his wife. Then at the end it was time for Dunstan to speak. His wife had been working hard, and he stood up in a spotless, crisply ironed surplice with a huge purple jewelled crucifix round his neck, looking, as he always did, immensely tall and cadaverous, but now also saintly. He spoke at length about the Christian values of pity for those who suffer and toleration of other people's views, of non-condemnation, of forgiveness and love. It was extraordinarily impressive. I was almost in tears of admira-

tion and gratitude; it was an aesthetically superb performance, and his words were greeted with total silence. He is, in
my view, a great man.

I was lucky in the members of the reconstituted committee,
with the appointment of whom I had had nothing whatever
to do. One was a cousin and former pupil of mine, Jane
Lloyd, whom I had hardly seen since she was an undergraduate, but whom I always greatly liked. She was now
married to an extremely attractive high court judge, and was
herself a JP. Then there was an amiable vet from Oxford,
whose children had been at school with mine, and who
looked after our cats; and an extraordinarily clever and nice
professor of pharmacology from Oxford, Bill Paton. The odd
man out was from the RSPCA, by repute a good zoologist.
But she had the ability, which I have never known in anyone
else, to pass out in a faint when she was losing an argument.
This was useful from her point of view, in that it caused such
a distraction that by the time she had come round and we
had all settled down again, it seemed impossible to go back
to where we had left the debate, and we moved on to the
next point. This happened three or four times.

Several Home Office inspectors sat in, in a dour row at the
back of our meetings, helpful enough with facts and figures,
if appealed to, but forming a rather daunting block. The
Home Office people (and this included the inspectorate)
were deeply suspicious of the proposed new legislation; and
though I tried, I could not see that this was for any reason
except that it would be new, though one of the civil servants
took me aside one day and told me that I must realize that
the inspectors thought that all the safeguards we were trying
to get into the bill were designed not so much to protect the
laboratory animals as to denigrate and belittle the current
work of the inspectorate.

I first met David Mellor in connection with this committee, he being then at the Home Office. Then and later I got on with him very well and liked him. He was remarkably enthusiastic about the legislation, and about the prospect of having a sound system of regulating research that could be the envy of other countries; and he was determined that our committee should continue to work after the current task was done, and gradually turn into a standing Advisory Committee on Animals, with a wider remit, an idea, he said, much resisted by the Home Office. At any rate our report was accepted by government. Then there was a long delay, mostly brought about by various directives from the European Commission, with which luckily the committee did not have to tangle. Finally, the Animals (Scientific Procedures) Bill was enacted in 1986.

I had told David Mellor that I did not want to stay on as chairman for very long, and he promised to find someone to replace me. But quite properly he wanted someone who would be seen not to have too great a stake in research using animals, so Richard Adrian would not do. We struggled on for a few years, trying to find ways of measuring stress in animals, rather than pain. This involved numerous visits to laboratories, which, on the whole, I enjoyed, and I came to admire particularly the Chief Inspector (Dr Rankin), a very sagacious and experienced Scot, who was authoritative and knowledgeable and genuinely fond of animals. I liked the visits except for the smell. Apart from the smell of horses, which I love, I am not tolerant of the smell of other animals, and once when visiting some beagles who were being used to test various tobacco-substitutes, I was nearly overcome by the smell (though the beagles were well looked after, and seemed to be enjoying themselves). I survived only by thinking of the terrible publicity there would be if the chairman of the committee actually passed out on being led into the lab. But the work of the committee by now seemed sporadic and a bit pointless. Nothing much would come of our attempts to define stress, and we were scraping around for other issues to examine.

One day in 1984 I was rung up by the philosopher Bernard Williams, who asked whether I thought he would enjoy being chairman of the committee, because he was going to have lunch with David Mellor to discuss it. I was as encouraging as I could be; but nothing came of it. At last in 1986 the extremely agreeable lawyer David Williams, who was to be the next Vice-Chancellor of Cambridge, and to stay on in that post, as it turned out, for longer than the then statutory two years, agreed to take over the committee, and I was off the hook. The new law was by now on the statute book, and among its provisions was the setting up of an advisory committee called the Animal Procedures Committee, into which our old committee was transformed. It was of this committee that David Williams became the chairman. Meanwhile, I was increasingly involved in publicizing the issues that had been debated in the Committee on Human Fertilization and Embryology, whose report had been published in 1984, but whose recommendations, as I have explained in Chapter 2, were still being widely debated; and so I put all the arguments about laboratory animals behind me, and forgot them. (I think people do not generally realize how easy it is to do this; unlike domestic and sentimental commitments, commitments that have been undertaken in response to governmental summonses can be as easily given up as they were once undertaken. I feel a sense of bewilderment when people assume that I still feel passionately committed to the rights of the disabled, or the needs of the infertile, or indeed the treatment of laboratory animals, though I have come back to that after a gap of fifteen years.)

Meanwhile, the 1986 Act was working reasonably well. But the extremist Animal Rights groups were becoming more active and more violent. In order, perhaps, to pacify them, the Labour Party manifesto of 1997, the year of their triumph, contained the promise to set up ethical review processes in every laboratory, whether in universities or in commercial companies, which used animals for research. Whatever form they took, these ethical scrutinizing bodies should be made up of both scientists and non-scientists, and should examine every application for a licence to use animals for research purposes, before the application was sent off to the Home Office Inspectorate.

This promise, however, and indeed its fulfilment, failed to satisfy the extremists whose attacks on individuals and on laboratories (notoriously the laboratory at Huntingdon, outside Cambridge) were becoming a form of terrorism that could not be ignored. Moreover the kinds of uses to which experimental animals might be put were changing. On the one hand it was increasingly possible to use human tissue for research into the development of drugs at a microbiological level. It was also possible to model animal reactions by computer. Such techniques, if they could be further developed, would reduce the need for the use of live animals. On the other hand, the growth of genetic engineering, and the targeting of specific drugs onto specific genes, requires animal trials, and such trials have substantially increased the number of animals used. Moreover, the European Commission has attempted to introduce widespread regulations for the use of animals in the toxicity-testing of household products not previously tested.

One way and another, it seemed to be time for a further examination of the issues surrounding the uses of animals for research. And so a House of Lords select committee was proposed, which would look into these issues, and would consider whether the 1986 Act was still adequate, or whether it should be amended, to bring it up to date. This select committee, of which I became a member, started to meet in the summer of 2001.

As I write, the committee has not yet reported. Indeed we are only just beginning to draft our report. But the Prime Minister, probably not even knowing of the existence of a committee about to report to parliament, has already made his views clear: the progress of science must not be impeded by any sentimentality about animals; protesters will be firmly dealt with; medical advances and the pharmaceutical companies must be supported. This is a view which is not incompatible with his former determination to have new ethical scrutiny of the use of animals in laboratories. Indeed, he may feel that, having put that in place and thus, as he hopes, reassured the animal-loving public, he is now free to offer his support to the scientists. The select committee, for its part, not being under the constraint of working in the setting of the Home Office, is able to take a far wider-ranging view than the committee that I chaired all those years ago (which, as I have noted above, still exists under the title The Animal Procedures Advisory Committee). Our task at that time was to propose legislative regulation that should govern all research using animals. We were, as I have said, essentially concerned with establishing a bureaucratic framework within which responsible work using animals could proceed.

The select committee, in contrast, is specifically concerned with considering the changed circumstances of animal research, its new methods and its new uses. Although it has been a condition of issuing a project licence since 1986 that the applicant should have given consideration to whether there were any alternatives to the use of animals for the proposed research, and the so-called three Rs (Replacement, Reduction and Refinement) are written into the Act as part of the goal of every licence-holder, the new alternatives are not given very high priority in the thinking either of most laboratories or of the Home Office Inspectorate, or so it has seemed to me. There is still too much emphasis on reducing the numbers of animals used, as though this were an adequate way of reducing the aggregate of suffering, a concept I still find pretty well meaningless.

The select committee has been able to take a great deal of oral as well as written evidence, and the oral evidence from the Home Office, who have been invited to see us twice, once at the beginning and once near the end of our evidence, has seemed to me defensive, conservative and complacent. It is rather like talking to someone high up in the BBC, absolutely certain that our television is the best in the world, or that no other country has anything to rival Radio 4. It may be so, we would like to believe it. But the evidence has come pouring in from scientists, who tell us that the bureaucracy is intolerable; that the time taken to process a licence application is twice as long as in any other country; that every least detail has to be included in the project licence; and that if the smallest change is to be made in the protocol (for example a change from the use of one strain of mouse to another, or a variation in the method of dosing the animals) a new licence must be applied for, thus wasting weeks of research time. Sometimes foreign visitors, respected and experienced practitioners in their own countries, have not time to get a licence to do the research they had planned before they have to go home again, or, if they do get one, they have to go through a training programme suitable for a first-time licence-holder. The Home Office inspectors, when we put these points to them, blamed the scientists for giving them more detail than they need on the application form for a licence, and claimed that this is what causes the delay. But in fact the application forms demand detail, and would be sure to be sent back if they were not completed properly.

None of this bureaucracy seems to have much effect on the welfare of the animals to be used, though doubtless it creates an atmosphere of strict adherence to the rules, which were originally drawn up to prevent the abuse of animals. But if scientists are not to be compelled to take their work abroad to escape the bureaucracy, it is essential, in my view, that there should be more trust between them and the Home Office, or more concession on the part of the Home Office that a senior scientist can control his own laboratory. This sort of trust is remarkably absent in this country, though not (as we saw on our travels) either in the United States or in France. Yet there was no evidence that in those countries the animals were any worse off.

There is notoriously a lack of trust of scientists, not only from the Home Office but from the public at large. The assumption is that only those who are not scientists care about the welfare of laboratory animals; that, if left to themselves, scientists would conduct experiments without any regard to the suffering that they might cause. This is manifestly untrue. Those who work most closely with the animals, both scientists and technicians, care most that they should be healthy and content, and have better ways of telling whether or not they are so. After all, to put it at its lowest, animals that are well looked after are better experimental material that those that are stressed or suffering ill-health. Every effort is made, in most laboratories, to give animals something approaching an environment in which they will flourish.

Some people argue that, if only scientists were less secretive, if only they dared to raise their heads above the parapet, and invite people into their laboratories, or otherwise publicize what they are doing, the public would cease to demonize them. I do not believe that this is true. It is not merely that there are obstacles in the way of spreading information about animal experiments that may be part of the development of a particular drug, the nature of which must remain a trade secret; it is also that, for many people who are hostile to the very idea of using animals for toxicity-testing or for experimental purpose, to see the animals being subjected to such tests and experiments, even though they might be anaesthetized and suffering no pain at all, would simply increase their opposition. For it is not so much the particular procedures that they object to (though in their propaganda they often emphasize the precise things that they allege are done to the animals), as the very idea that animals should be used at all in laboratories. The more they saw of the rats and mice, marmosets and rabbits in their cages, the more outraged they would become.

Another issue with which the select committee has been concerned is the so-called cost/benefit analysis that is used in the decision-making about any research project that is proposed. This analysis has nothing to do with resources. It is a weighing up of the probable 'cost' in terms of the suffering of animals against the probable 'benefit' to animals, but especially human animals, that is likely to flow from the research. Now this is plainly a matter of guesswork. It is true that some research has been generally banned in the UK, such as research using animals that is targeted to the development of cosmetics (though the individual ingredients of the cosmetics will probably have been tested on animals), on the vague grounds that such research is frivolous, or 'not worth it'. And this vague criterion is about all that can be forthcoming, in the cost/benefit analysis. For much of the research that goes on, not just in university laboratories but within the pharmaceutical companies, is designed to increase knowledge, for instance of how a particular gene is expressed, or what will be the consequences of 'blocking' or eliminating a gene. New knowledge of this kind may or may not lead to medical benefits in the long run, and whether it will or not must be a matter of judgement. Such judgements are not to be despised; indeed they are an essential part of the business of assessing research projects. But they should not be presented as more accurate, less subjective, than they are.

A further issue that has occupied the select committee is that of the role of the newly formed 'ethical review process', now mandatory for every laboratory using animals. Apart from aiming to reassure the public, part of the purpose of these bodies was to be to shorten the time taken for an application for a project licence to go through the Inspectorate. For before the local ethical review processes were set up, it was the inspectors who had to assess the ethical acceptability of the research that was proposed. However, as far as we could see, though the local ethical people give advice to scientists about how to present their applications so that they are clear and unambiguous, many experienced scientists hardly need this advice. Moreover, the proposed application may take up to eight weeks to be cleared by the local ethical group, and the time taken by the Inspectorate to approve the application has not been reduced. There seems thus to be another layer of bureaucracy added to the whole process, with no gains. Nor do I think that the public is likely to be much reassured by this newly established check on the scientists, since they probably know little about it. I personally believe that to set up these bodies was one of Blair's ill-thought-through wheezes that has turned out to do no good at all, and perhaps harm.

All these issues, and more, were the concern of the select committee. And because we were able to put questions to those whom we called to give evidence, including, besides the Home Office officials, numerous scientists, antivivisectionists, journalists and others, we were constantly thinking not only about the issues but about our own beliefs. When some of us visited the United States, besides seeing several laboratories and talking to people about the regulation of research (as I have said, much more relaxed than in this country), we also talked to Peter Singer, a philosopher now at Princeton University, and previously Director of the Center for Human Bioethics at Monash University. Singer, though he did not invent the term, has concentrated in much of his writing on the evils of speciesism. Bentham, as far as I know, was the first to raise the question of whether other animals than humans should be taken into account in the calculation of pleasures and pains that in his view formed the sole criterion of the difference between right and wrong. He wrote 'The question is not Can they reason? Nor Can they talk? But Can they suffer?' And he went on:

> The French have already discovered that the blackness of the skin is no reason why a human being should be abandoned without redress to the caprice of a tormentor. It may one day come to be recognized that the number of legs, the villosity of the skin or the termination of the os sacrum are reasons equally

insufficient for abandoning a sensitive creature to the same fate.*

Singer, following Bentham's passing thought, wrote this:

> Where animals and humans have similar interests –
> and we might take the interest in avoiding physical
> pain as an example, for it is an interest that humans
> clearly share with other animals – those interests are to
> be counted equally, with no automatic discount, just
> because one of the beings is not human.

The argument against giving humans priority, Singer told us, is that there are no characteristics to which we can point that would mark off humans from other animals. The more we know about the capacities of dolphins or chimpanzees, the less we can think of a total discontinuity between human and other abilities. And what are we to say about those humans who, while manifestly members of the species *homo sapiens*, not only show no signs of reason but will never be able to do so, because of the damage their brain has suffered, perhaps at birth. Singer asks,

> why do we lock up chimpanzees in appalling primate
> research centers and use them in experiments that
> range from the uncomfortable to the agonizing and
> lethal yet would never think of doing the same to a
> retarded human being at a much lower mental level?
> ... There is no ethical basis for elevating membership
> of one particular species into a morally crucial

---

* Jeremy Bentham, *Principles of Morals and Legislation* (London, 1822), Chapter 17, section 1, note.

characteristic. From an ethical point of view we all stand on an equal footing whether we stand on two feet or four or none at all.†

Singer is not always quite so radical. In other places, and in his conversation with the select committee, he distinguished between 'persons' and 'non-persons'. Persons are those who take a conscious pleasure in their lives and therefore should not be prematurely deprived of life. This category includes human beings (though not neonates or the severely mentally incompetent) and also certain animals, chimpanzees and dolphins certainly, though he is doubtful about pigs, and certainly excludes flatworms and tadpoles, wasps and mosquitoes. This latter exclusion is useful to him. For frequently in conversation with those opposed to the use of animals in research we asked our interlocutors where they drew the line in the sensitivity of animals, and their right not to be used for human purposes. They were mostly exceedingly unwilling to answer this question. Some said, 'Well, we're pragmatists. We just want to put an end to the suffering of those animals that are currently kept and used in laboratories. Don't ask us hypothetical questions about how we would respond to research using flat-worms or fruit-flies.' I felt strongly that they ought to have been prepared to answer the question. Singer, however, has an answer. He does not defend all animals, only those he has deemed to be persons. But it has to be said that his criterion of personhood is not only vague but fraught with subjectivism. He relies, in the case of chimpanzees on their mental ability and their similarities to humans, as well as their developed social life,

---

† Peter Singer, *Practical Ethics* (Cambridge: Cambridge University Press, 1979), Chapter 3.

in the wild. Dolphins, too, get in on account of the size of their brains. But pigs? It seems that he has a fondness for pigs, but does not much care for horses, who are excluded. I would, if I were tempted to use such a criterion, certainly count them in. They undoubtedly have personalities, and often, as when fox-hunting or racing, appear to enjoy themselves and therefore, I suppose, could be said to value being alive.

But redefining personhood does not really constitute an argument. It seems to me that Singer, in asserting that chimpanzees are persons in a way that neonates or the mentally disabled are not, is simply repeating his intuition that it is wrong to use, at any rate some, intelligent animals for research purposes, or, presumably, to eat them. And by implication he is saying that if we could get results from research that used defective neonates, or other non-persons such as horses, it would be all right to use them for this purpose, as long as the results were of benefit to those who were persons, chimpanzees, for example, and the rest of us. But since his definition of personhood is so difficult to apply (do we know, for example, that ants are not persons? They certainly lead an orderly and social life), we cannot successfully derive the argument against research using certain animals from this definition, or if we do, the argument will be circular.

In conversation with Singer, or with other people opposed to the use of animals for research, it is often difficult to avoid confusion between two different things which should be distinguished. There is a difference between objecting to research using animals on the ground that it causes pain to those who can feel it (and this includes far more than Singer's persons, it certainly includes rabbits, rats and mice, and even, possibly, crustaceans and fish), and objecting to using animals for research even where the procedures are carried out under anaesthetic, and the animal is killed at the end of the experiment, perhaps not being allowed to recover. The first is a straightforward argument such as Bentham might have used, that it is morally wrong to cause pain, where pain can be experienced. The second is an argument against exploitation: we should not use other species for our own ends, even if they suffer no pain. The first would be the kind of argument used by someone who was a vegetarian because he believed that fattening animals for the table and slaughtering them causes them suffering. The second would be used by a vegetarian who said, 'It is wrong to eat other animals, even if their slaughter is completely painless.' This is the more radical argument, and is based on the thought, shared, for example by Buddhists, who think that all living creatures are to be respected and preserved.

According to the first argument, pain and perhaps stress and anxiety, put together under the general category of 'suffering' is the only thing that matters. If suffering is somehow eliminated for the animal, death does not matter, provided of course that death itself is not painful. On the whole those who call themselves animal welfarists take this line. Since laboratory mice are bred for the laboratory, and are not an endangered species, the humane killing of mice is not to be weighed in the cost/benefit calculation. Only their suffering, if any, is to be put in the balance. According to the second argument, presumably the premature death of any animal is a cost to be taken into account. This would mean that animals should not be used at all in laboratories, for they will certainly end up dead. This confusion is reflected, in my view, in the thought that the number of animals used in experiments is important, and it is almost the only thing intelligibly shown in the Home Office statistics.

All these arguments show conclusively, in my view, that we simply do think of ourselves as importantly different from other animals. This is brought out especially in the view that the death of an animal is not to be weighed in the cost/benefit calculation. For such a view suggests that the animal that has been humanely killed can be easily replaced by another, perhaps to repeat the experiment, perhaps to go on to the next stage. But in the case of human beings, any human beings, we do not for one moment think that one will replace another. Unless we cease to think of them as human, and think instead of their being soldiers in the trenches, mere cannon-fodder, we are bound to think of each one that has been killed as having his own unique value, both to us and to himself. He had his own life which has been cut short. Moreover, as I have said, humans suffer more if they realize that others are suffering with them, that they are part of an unjust purge, or a mass starvation. The same is not true of mice. A mouse suffers perhaps and dies, with no thought of the wrong that has been done him. We, as humans, then, simply do accord a higher value to our own species than to others. To argue, as Bentham did, that we have gradually extended our sympathies beyond our families, fellow tribes-men or countrymen to other races, and those who live at a distance from us, is simply to reinforce the argument that we have gradually come to feel more sympathy with and responsibility for humanity as a whole. It tells us nothing about our duty to embrace on equal terms all other species of animal, or even those specially favoured animals we might like to call persons.

Speciesism, then, is not the name of a prejudice which we should try to wipe out. It is not a kind of injustice. It is a natural consequence of the way we and our ancestors have established the institution of society, within which the concepts of right and wrong, and the law, have their meaning. The myth of the Creation, with man as the dominant species in charge of the rest, did not form our attitudes. It is rather a storybook expression of existing attitudes, as is the way with myths.

But of course to say that we inevitably give preference to our own species does not entitle us to be indifferent to the sufferings of the rest. On the contrary. Only human beings are capable of a conscious, principled morality. Only they are deliberate moral agents (and it is partly this fact, no doubt, that gives them their unique value). But this does not entail that only other humans can be beneficiaries of the moral principles they have devised. It is simply not the case that to benefit from the principles of a moral agent you need to be a moral agent yourself. So for example we have obligations to look after infants who are not moral agents. Similarly I believe that if we need for our own generally beneficent ends (for medical purposes, that is) to use animals in research, we have obligations to treat those animals well, and ameliorate, as far as possible, the sufferings we might impose on them. This, I take it, is the belief of those who are concerned with the welfare of animals in laboratories, or by analogy in farms or racing stables, come to that. This I believe is the consensus among members of the select committee, and of most of those who gave evidence to it.

The reason that this committee is such fun is that it is possible, indeed necessary, to discuss these fundamental issues. It is also fun, it has to be said, because we have a sardonic, outspoken, sometimes slightly sharp chairman in Lord Smith of Guildford, and many other clever and talkative members. Our trip to the United States was enormously enjoyable, and I look back on it as a time of endless laughter. We had allotted to us from the British Embassy in Washington an American girl called Julie who came everywhere with us to look after all our arrangements, tickets, travel and timetable. She was, we learned, a space scientist with nothing else to do at the time. She was exceedingly thin and pale, and wore quite smart town clothes and the most enormous pair of white trainers on her feet. She hardly ever spoke, whereas we were often quite noisy on our bus journeys; we had in our party the Earl of Onslow, an ebullient companion, given to outrageous remarks, and irrepressibly talkative, who wears colourful shirts and bow-ties and brilliant socks. He also had a splendid overcoat with a great cape, and looked decidedly un-American. He is an excellent member of the committee, though the chairman has sometimes to suppress him. But he is unafraid to ask questions of a fundamental and probing nature; he is very bright at perceiving the implications of the answers he gets, and he has endless curiosity about the subject.

Another member who came on the American trip was Lord Soulsby, a retired vet, and therefore a good person to have in our visits to laboratories. I caught him in one occasion, in a rather smelly laboratory, overcrowded with rodents, running his finger along a shelf like a critical mother-in-law, and looking equally disapproving. There was also Lady Eccles, extraordinarily charming, funny and sympathetic. All in all we got on so well with one another, and had so much time to talk about what we had seen and heard that we feared that when we got back the rest of the committee would seem left out. But it did not turn out like that. I was deeply disappointed not to be able to join the expedition to France, because I longed for another, though shorter, time both for learning and for conversation, but I had a tedious lecture to give at the time.

Another delight of this committee, in contrast to other government or ministerial committees I have had to do with, is the outstanding excellence of the clerk, Thomas Elias. There is no doubt that clerks in the House of Lords are quite exceptionally bright. He is very young, and read music at Cambridge, but nothing scientific seems too much for him. His office is near mine, in Millbank House, across the road from the House of Lords, and we quite often meet and discuss the business, usually ending in laughter. One way and another, it will be a sad day when 'Animals' disappears as an entry in my diary. Whether what we recommend will make any difference to the practices of the Home Office is more than doubtful; but at least for us, the committee, we will greatly have clarified our ideas.

# 5  Administration of the Arts

If I try to imagine a world in which I am completely blind and completely deaf (and there are children who are born in this state), it strikes me that my life would be so amazingly much poorer than it is and has been, that I cannot conceive that it would be worth living. This is of course partly to do with the immense practical difficulties that there would be in living an everyday life; but it is more that the whole dimension of life that is broadly comprehended under the heading 'the aesthetic' (of which the arts form a part) would be absent. I could not hear music; I could not see landscape, or pictures or architecture; I could not, even if I learned to read Braille, understand the cadences and music-like rhythms of poetry or, indeed, of prose. My life, difficult enough at a practical level, would be lived entirely on the surface.

Now this may be an exaggeration. There may exist ways of feeling, and of expressing feeling, that I have been unable to imagine. There may be compensatory sensitivities in the sense of touch, or smell, for example, which, we are often told, do exist, and yield up pleasures to those who are born blind, pleasures and understanding which the sighted cannot comprehend. But my own failure to see the point of a life without hearing or sight at least suggests the crucial importance of these senses for those who are not thus deprived. And this, in turn, suggests that the aesthetic, including literary, visual and musical, arts are central to my life and the lives of those who, like me, take for granted the pleasures of these senses.

It may seem an exaggeration, and a pretentious one at that, to say that the arts are central to the life of someone who has, as I have, no particular artistic talents, who seldom goes either to the theatre or to picture galleries, who no longer plays any musical instrument in a recognizably decent way, and who attempts no kind of 'creative writing'. Yet there is something here that is crucial to the manner in which we, as human beings, distinct from other animals, conduct ourselves. Other animals express their feelings, fear, enjoyment, protectiveness of their offspring, sexual attraction and desire. But only humans do so self-consciously, knowing that there is a universality in these feelings and their expression, uniquely able to find ways to express them in the absence of their immediate trigger, to reproduce them and lay them down as something that will survive and be passed on from one generation to another.

Whatever debates there may be about the proper relationship between human beings and other animals, whatever objections may be raised to regarding humans as in some way superior to the rest, it is an undoubted truth that only humans indulge in art. Only humans have a sense of the passage of time, and therefore the desire to enshrine some things as worth, as it were, framing to be contemplated as monuments that will survive the endless destruction of time. The arts, I believe, necessarily look for a kind of permanence, even if they often fail to achieve it. And so, for people like me who are in no sense artists, enjoying the works of people who are, art gives a sense of immortality, and of a significance to life quite different from the significance that derives from our immediate mundane plans and projects. There is, it is true, a significance or purposefulness to one's life that comes from saying, on waking up, 'Today I have got to teach these people; post this letter; weed this bed in the garden.' And it is possible to live for days or weeks, or probably for ever, at this level of significance. But if one is occasionally prone to raise the question what is the point of all this bustle, or what else is there to think about, if these day-to-day tasks suddenly begin to seem boring or futile, or impossible, through the debility of age, to carry out, then it is the arts (or religion, which I regard among the most deeply aesthetic concepts that we have) that will supply an answer, and an assurance that nothing need ever be boring or futile. We can always give it significance, by wallowing (and I use this word without pejorative meaning) in the sensibilities and probably ineffable insights provided by music, poetry, novels, or (less certainly, for me) paintings.

In his autobiography, John Stuart Mill described how, when he was a young man, he became acutely depressed. All the great causes that he had hitherto embraced, including the bettering of the world according to utilitarian principles, suddenly seemed to him futile. He was still intellectually convinced that the feelings that arose from the pursuit of the good of others were the greatest and surest source of happiness: 'But to know that a feeling would make me happy if I had it did not give me the feeling.' He seemed to have no feelings at all. What gradually pulled him out of this dark tunnel was the poetry of Wordsworth:

> What made Wordsworth's poems a medicine for my state of mind was that they expressed not mere outward beauty, but states of feeling, and of thought coloured by feeling, under the excitement of beauty.

180

They seemed to be the very culture of the feelings which I was in quest of. In them I seemed to draw from a source of inward joy, of sympathetic and imaginative pleasure which could be shared by all human beings; from them I seemed to learn what would be the perennial sources of happiness, even when all the greater evils of life shall have been removed.*

I am not suggesting that the value of art is therapeutic. It may be so, and it proved so in Mill's case. But the manner in which Wordsworth's poetry was therapeutic for Mill demonstrates that the aesthetic has an intrinsic and irreplaceable value for us, and can make our lives seem to have a significance, a point, as nothing else can.

However, when the Arts Council was set up in 1945 its aim could indeed be seen as therapeutic. It took over from a wartime institution, the Council for the Encouragement of Music and the Arts (CEMA) which had been funded by the Pilgrim Trust, and was specifically intended to raise people's courage at a time when, to quote Maynard Keynes's words, 'all sources of comfort to our spirits were at a low ebb'. Keynes, in his broadcast announcing the inauguration of the Arts Council, said, 'At last the public exchequer has recognized the support and encouragement of the civilizing arts as part of their duty.' Support for the arts became, in fact, part of the function of the new Welfare State. But, according to Keynes, the arts must not be 'socialized', as medicine or pensions had been. Artists must be left to do whatever they liked. 'New work will spring up more abundantly in unexpected quarters and in unforessen shapes when there is a

---

* John Stuart Mill, *Autobiography* (London: Oxford University Press, 1924), p. 112.

universal opportunity for contact with traditional and con-
temporary arts in their noblest forms.'

Since then, every government has felt it necessary to
recognize the duty of subsidizing the arts. Of course
patronage for the arts existed long before 1945. Artists were
commissioned, their work subsidized, from ancient Greek
and Roman times onwards. But patronage, before the
twentieth century, most commonly arose out of a desire to
celebrate some period of success and grandeur. Thus
Augustus commissioned Vergil to write a Homeric epic to
celebrate the newly flourishing empire; and the rebuilding of
Rome at the same time was specifically intended to be a vast
monument to the values of that empire. People had only to
look around them to see the achievements. And the same had
been true of Periclean Athens. The rich, too, had always been
able to exercise private patronage. What was new in the
twentieth century was the necessity, as it was felt to be, for
every government to have a policy for the arts. And with this
public policy there grew up a special kind of bureaucracy,
known as arts administration, a monstrous growth, it seems,
attracting to itself people who are art lovers but not practitioners, a peculiar and distinctive breed of civil servants.

Arts administration is that species of bureaucracy that is
concerned not with creating art, nor even, usually, with
commissioning it, but with distributing money to artists and
arranging that other people can benefit from their work. It is
an essentially second-order activity, parasitic on the real
imaginative business of the arts.

There is a good deal of overlap between the organization
of the arts and that of education. Both could be said to exist
in order to enable people to do things and enjoy things they
would not be able to do or enjoy without help. When people
sometimes complain that museums and galleries these days

pay too much attention to education in arranging the contents of the museum or setting up exhibitions, what they usually mean is that the education of children has been unduly emphasized, thus rendering the exhibition unsuitable for grown-ups, too patronizing, too explicitly informative. But in another sense, every curator must hope to educate the public, opening their eyes to new insights, expanding their imaginative horizons, just as everyone who puts on a concert must hope that by the end people will have learned something, having experiences they have never exactly had before. My own first encounter with arts administration was, unsurprisingly, within the limited field of education, specifically music education.

In the early 1960s I became a member of the Oxfordshire LEA, at that time separate from the City of Oxford, and serving a predominantly rural county. It was their custom to have a member of the university on the LEA, and I was there in that capacity. It was a totally non-political body (unlike the city LEA), and indeed no one with any political ambitions would have wanted to serve on it. It was, however, a body seriously devoted to the education of children, and all members gave considerable time to their work.

The chairman under whom I first served was Jack Peers, who could, I suppose, have been described as a 'gentleman farmer'. He lived in a beautiful large house in Chiselhampton, a few miles from Oxford. I knew him already, since we were both governors of the Oxford High School (before I became headmistress), and one of his daughters was a friend of my eldest daughter at their primary school, and she used to come to stay with us in our Yorkshire holiday house. He was succeeded as chairman by Jack Cooper, a panel basher from the then flourishing

Cowley works. (Both Peers and Cooper now have schools named after them in the county.)

The chief executive, the Director of Education, was a reclusive and mysterious man called Mr Chorlton. He had a scarred face, and the scar used to intensify in colour when he was vexed or put out, which was often, since he was shy to the point of paralysis. Nevertheless, he was educationally highly imaginative, and could get his way with the county council. Oxfordshire became famous at this time, both for the eagerness with which primary schools turned into child-centred gardens, where children could grow and flourish, discovering things (like how to read) for themselves, rather than being taught them, according to the new orthodoxy of the Plowden Report, and for the speed with which grammar schools were abolished and all secondaries except one in the whole county became comprehensive schools. All this, for good or ill, was done at the insistence of Mr Chorlton. There was plenty of money to spend, and the provision of music, with free instrumental lessons for all children who wanted them, was part of the generous plan.

But here the trouble began. The Director of Music for the county was a most surprising person. She was called Constance Pilkington, generally known to both children and colleagues as 'The Pilk.' She was a member of the wealthy glass-manufacturing family from Liverpool, and, though only in her early fifties at this time, had neatly cut, snow-white hair and piercing blue eyes. She walked as old-fashioned ladies (including my mother) did, with her toes turned out. And she wore the most exquisite, highly polished lace-up shoes, of which she always had three pairs in her car, in case one should get muddy on her trips round the schools, which she made tirelessly. She wore beautiful stripey Macclesfield silk shirts, and well-tailored tweed skirts. I once, in a

184

moment of unusual intimacy, said how much I admired her shoes. 'Where do you get them?' I innocently asked. She looked deeply offended, and, after a pause, said, 'I have them made for me, of course.' She was profoundly interested in children's music, had very demanding standards, and an infallible ear for who was a talented or even a reasonably promising musician. Her disadvantage as an administrator, however, was her total inability to see the wood for the trees. I have never known anybody for whom this metaphor was more apt.

When the time came each year to set the budget for the next year, and The Pilk was summoned to explain the needs of music, she came in with her hands full of random bits of paper, her expression a mixture of anxiety and disdain, and she would embark on a flow of words: 'Valerie will have to pull out of the violin-teaching at Henley; Elizabeth can't be expected to take all the clarinettists at Bicester; there is no brass teacher to cover Witney; they are short of music-stands at Wallingford ...' The Director of Education was beside himself. He was inclined to abolish music altogether rather than try to make sense of this rigmarole. So Jack Peers, who was proud of the county music, decided to establish a music sub-committee to oversee music provision in the county and report to the LEA, and produce a budget. I was to be chairman, and The Pilk was to attend every meeting. There were also to be external members. The plan was put into operation and was a great success.

We had three outside members, a retired music critic from *The Times*, the organist and choirmaster of Magdalen College, and Jean Maud, the wife of the Master of University College, a former concert pianist, and previously involved with the rural music schools, and so accustomed to encouraging amateur music and to providing concerts in schools and village halls. She still played the piano with wild abandon, most notably at soirées at University College, where she used to crash out the Rachmaninov, while her husband, the most discreet of men, used to tiptoe round replenishing the glasses of the guests. (It was of John Maud that Maurice Bowra said, 'With him you have to learn to take the smooth with the smooth.') When the golden age of county music was beginning to pass, and economies were called for, it was decreed that when instrumentalists went round to primary schools to demonstrate their instruments and introduce them to the children, they might no longer have an accompanist. So Jean Maud used to go round with them, unpaid, and play accompaniments, no doubt to the detriment of the school pianos, and reward the instrumentalists afterwards with a magnificent lunch in the college. She was a proper trooper, undaunted by mud or fog or rain.

Bernard Rose, the organist of Magdalen, was equally generous of his time. He used to spend many hours auditioning students for scholarships which enabled them to buy their own instruments, or go to London for instrumental lessons on Saturday mornings. And he attended endless end-of-term concerts where the awards were given out. I greatly enjoyed my part in all these activities. Bernard Rose much admired The Pilk for her high standards and good judgement. But he and I used to puzzle about her reticence about what she had actually studied in her days at the Royal College. We guessed that it might have been piano; but she never told anyone, and never played any instrument, in her days as Director of Music.

But the music flourished. There seemed for a time in the 1960s to be no limit to the money that could be spent. The Saturday morning school provided not only an excellent orchestra, conducted by such people as Muir Matheson, the conductor of film music, who had conducted Walton's music for the film of *Henry V*, among other things, and then his brother, John, a marvellous musician who was even better with children than Muir. It was an exciting time; and the youngest four of my own children greatly benefited from all that went on. The Pilk retired just about the time when the great educational spending spree came to an end, in the mid-1970s. Though county music struggled on, it was never quite the same again.

However, my contact with her was not over. When I was at Girton, I was, as usual, trying to raise money for the college, and I wrote to the Pilkington family trust to appeal to them to contribute funds. One of the early members of the college had married into the family, and one of their daughters had also been a Girtonian. They had already given generously to the college, especially in funding the construction of a pretty court in the middle of the college buildings. In writing to ask them to contribute again, I added, as an afterthought, that the daughter of the original Girtonian whom I had known best had not been at Cambridge, but at the Royal College of Music, and that I had worked closely with her, and had always admired her sensitive interest in the needs of young musicians. (This was The Pilk. I did not even know whether she was still alive.)

The Pilkington family responded generously. But suddenly one day I was rung up by an unknown Liverpool solicitor who said that he had been instructed by his client, Miss Constance Pilkington, to call on me in Girton. It turned out that The Pilk was in a nursing home in Hertfordshire, having suffered a stroke. She had not spoken for two years, but she was still sent all the correspondence that came to the family trust, and she had read my letter. Upon which, to everyone's astonishment, she picked up the telephone and demanded that her solicitor come to see me, with a view to her donating money, from her private funds, to Girton, provided only that the money should go towards promoting music in the college. The solicitor arrived, having been asked to lunch. He was a man of few words. I had asked the Bursar to come to talk to him with me, but she was held up, and arrived late. By the time she came, everything had been settled. He said, 'What do you want?' And I said, extremely nervously, 'Well, what we would really like would be a contribution towards funding a fellowship in music.' (We had up to this time been unable to afford a fellow of our own, but had employed as a lecturer a fellow of Emmanuel, who had just been appointed to a senior post in her own college and was going to have to withdraw from her commitment to Girton.) So he said, 'What would it cost to endow a fellowship?' I named a large six-figure sum. He said, 'All right. That is what Miss Pilkington would like to give, as long as it is not called after her, but after her parents.' So by the time the Bursar arrived, the Austin and Hope Pilkington Fellowship had been agreed to. The Bursar had only to arrange how the money should be paid. If Girton can no longer afford to pay any of its fellows, this fellowship will remain. And in fact there was money left over to enable us to buy a wonderful harpsichord for the college. (The fellow we appointed was a harpsichordist.) I wrote to The Pilk to thank her, and again to tell her whom we had appointed, and to fill her in with the lives of all my children in whom she had been interested, and for whom she had done so much. But after about three months I learned that she died. I like to think that she went on doing good for music education and enabling other people to take part in and enjoy music to the very end of her life.

My next personal encounter with arts administration was also when I was in Cambridge. In the summer of 1987 I was asked to chair an internal committee (though with external membership) to inquire into the governance and finances of the Fitzwilliam Museum. This was a far less agreeable, and also less fruitful, undertaking than the Oxfordshire music sub-committee. The Fitzwilliam Museum was founded in 1816 by the bequest of Lord Fitzwilliam. Its palatial building was not completed until 1850, to the design of C. R. Cockerell (who had earlier won the competition to design the Ashmolean Museum in Oxford). The books, pictures and artifacts were arranged in 1849, though they were later rearranged by the extraordinarily interventionist Vice-Chancellor and Master of Trinity, the scientist and philosopher William Whewell, who seized the chance to hide in a remote gallery and behind curtains Fitzwilliam's collection of Venetian nudes. The museum is greatly extended today, and is of enormous value both to the university and to the public. This inquiry was my first encounter with the mysteries of curating.

The Fitzwilliam was one of a number of institutions in Cambridge (such as, for example, Fenners Sports Ground) which did not fall under any faculty, but which was yet the responsibility of the university. In my day there was a committee of which I was a member, and later chairman, called the Allocations Committee which, in an amazingly ramshackle and haphazard way, received some money from the treasurer and dished it out, trying in vain to meet all the conflicting demands, in accordance with no principle, but largely at the mercy of which institution could make itself most disagreeable if its demands were not met. The treasurer, a combative man called Michael Halstead, who had come to run the finances of Cambridge from the oil industry

(I think), was driven to distraction by the incompetence, ignorance and lack of financial sense both of the Allocations Committee and the committee (or syndicate) specifically charged with the finances of the Fitzwilliam which put in its demands each year to the Allocations Committee. It was perhaps to save his sanity that the committee of inquiry was set up.

The Fitzwilliam had other sources of funding, apart from the university, most notably the Fitzwilliam Museum Trust, a charitable body which had on its board several very successful fund-raisers, such as Mary Archer. But it was more interested, understandably, in new acquisitions than in the day-to-day costs of the museum, or even in crucial conservation. There was also a small income from the Friends of the Fitzwilliam, who among other things ran the profit-making shop and coffee shop. In addition the LEA contributed a small sum for the educational exhibitions that were laid on, though this grant was under threat. And in any case educational exhibitions, and free entry for school children, were frowned upon by the curator and by the Trust.

In the last analysis, the university was responsible for keeping the museum open and its contents in good shape. In the 1980s this was becoming a more and more impossible task. Nor were the difficulties entirely financial. There was a great deal of discontent among the staff, and one senior member, a keeper, had been on sick leave, and on full pay, for many months. It was a conspicuously unhappy ship.

The museum syndics (the members of the syndicate in charge of the Fitzwilliam) selected the external members of our committee of inquiry, and in this they showed extremely good judgement. During the committee's short lifetime, I came increasingly to rely on the dispassionate good sense of these members, who could distance themselves from the internal feuds of Cambridge. Among them was a nice man, Christopher White, already known to me, and much admired by Geoffrey, who was Director of the Ashmolean, the Fitzwilliam's counterpart in Oxford. And there was a charming and clever keeper from the British Museum, who is now Warden of Merton College, Oxford, Jessica Rawson. I recognized her at once when we had our first meeting; her maiden name was Quirk, and she came of a Winchester family, many of them, like her, conspicuously red-haired, who had been friends of my mother, and whose children, including her father, had been friends of my older siblings. I had last met her, I am ashamed to say, when she came for an interview at St Hugh's as a schoolgirl seeking to read Greats, and I had turned her down. I try to comfort myself that I did her a good turn. She went instead to London University and read oriental languages instead of classics. In this she became a notable scholar and a world expert in her field. She is now Dame Jessica. She was an enormous support to me in the traumas that lay ahead.

Our preliminary meeting, in July 1987, was traumatic enough. We were booked into a room already reserved by another committee, so we spent the first half hour trailing round the Old Schools in the pouring rain, looking for somewhere to meet. In the end we went into the Senate Room and sat round the enormous table at which the Senate met every Monday, peering at each other through the darkness (none could locate the light switches), unable to hear what was being said. It was a poor way to get to know each other. But I suppose we at least fixed the date of the next meeting.

Soon after that I had a note from the director of the museum, Michael Jaffé, saying that he had discovered that I lived in Wiltshire. He was to be in Dorset for part of the vacation, so he proposed to come over to visit me. Grudgingly,

191

I agreed and fixed a day in August for him to come to lunch at our house near Marlborough. Geoffrey was there at lunch, and we got through that pretty well with talk about Oxford and Cambridge, the Ashmolean and how it compared with the Fitzwilliam, and so on. Also I had made some rather good cold parsley and lemon soup which Jaffé thought amazingly clever and admirable, so, for the first and last time, I came in for some commendation. But Geoffrey left after coffee, and I was then subjected to a tirade about the iniquities of the setting-up of a committee of inquiry, and especially a committee of which he himself was not a member. I was told that it was only the stupidity and mean-mindedness of the university that prevented the Fitzwilliam from being not only the greatest but the best-run museum in Europe, if not in the world. Its pre-eminence would of course be recognized worldwide if he, Jaffé, were permitted to take exhibitions not only to the United States (where an exhibition was indeed going at vast expense in the following year), but to Japan, Latin America, Russia and so on. I had nothing to say, and in any case would not have been able to get a word in if I had wanted to. At about a quarter to five he jumped up and said he must go because his wife would be tired of waiting. It turned out that she had been sitting in the car at the bottom of our drive since half-past twelve. (I did not even know he had a wife or I would thankfully have invited her to lunch as well.)

The next term our proper meetings started. The first was a disaster. We had to be shown all round the museum, which was fine, except that it was Jaffé who showed us round, and we got no chance to talk to any of the keepers or librarians. Afterwards I had to ask him to allow us on future occasions to meet the staff on their own. He was furious. I was reminded of what my mother used to quote on such occasions: 'One more insult to Ireland'. Though he did more or less keep out of our way in future, we were always uneasily conscious that he might be lurking round the next corner or listening through the keyhole.

Apart from the keeper who was on sick-leave, there were other eccentric members of staff. I remember especially the librarian who had charge of the original Fitzwilliam books, housed in a beautiful panelled library of a circular design. He used to arrive at eight o'clock in the morning and depart late in the evening, never leaving the library all day. There were two or three books on display, but the rest were never touched. They had not been catalogued, and no one knew what they were or what treasures they contained. A few of them had had their leather bindings restored, but most, through lack of funds, were falling into decay.

In our investigations we saw everyone, from the keepers and the restorers to the boiler-men and people who served in the shop. We had numerous written submissions, including volumes from the poor man on sick-leave, and we heard a great deal of oral evidence. Towards the end of January 1988, we put aside a morning to interview Jaffé. (Mostly we interviewed people for an hour, finding that if they had more time they tended to repeat themselves.) We always prepared ahead the questions we wanted to ask of each witness, and sent them a copy of these in advance. I had the external members to stay in Girton the evening before Jaffé's evidence so that we could start at nine. We had a lunch engagement in Clare College at one.

I started out by apologizing for our list of questions being so long in this case, but said that, as we had four hours, we should get through them if we could allocate about a quarter of an hour to each. Some of them, I said, required only brief factual answers. (I think there were nineteen questions.) Of course I should have known what would happen. Instead of starting on the questions, Jaffé burst into a frenzied monologue, of a perfectly general nature, going over very much the same ground as he had covered in Wiltshire the summer before. I managed eventually to get him back to the questions. But by half-past twelve we had dealt with only three.

I was completely desperate. I realized that this was entirely my fault: I simply was not acting as a proper chairman. I finally managed to intervene to say that we had only half an hour left, and he must try to cover the remaining points in that time. Upon this he leapt to his feet, and leaned across the table shaking his papers in my face. He said, 'I will not be treated like this. How dare you interrupt me. I shall speak for as long as I choose.' I said, as coolly as I could manage, that we had a lunch engagement, and had arranged to see members of the Trust in the afternoon, so he must use the half hour as best he could. However, the ranting and shouting went on, and the time was dwindling away. So reluctantly, and feeling unutterably feeble, I said that he should write a paper which would cover the remaining points, and we would find an occasion to go through it with him when he had had time to write it and we to read it. And so it was left. I still do not know how I should or could have conducted the meeting. Strangely I did not get much sympathy from any of my colleagues except Jessica. I believe that people from Cambridge were accustomed to Jaffé's tantrums, and perhaps those better acquainted with the world of museums and galleries than I expect such prima donna-ish behaviour from curators and directors. At any rate when we got his paper, and fixed another meeting, he told us that he could give us only half an hour; and that passed off politely enough.

Jessica said, after the first meeting, that if she had been in my place she would have found herself bursting into tears. I

194

am sure she would not. But I realized when she said this that I felt relatively detached, like a spectator, because of the uncanny resemblance between Jaffé and my maternal grandfather, Felix Schuster, who was, like Jaffé, bearded and dark, with a pale melancholy face, and who was also prone to appalling outbursts of rage. My poor mother was terrified of him; and I suppose I was determined to be braver than she could ever be, even though not more effective.

Quite soon after that we started to draft our report, a list of recommendations for reorganization, better delegation, reforms in the interests of economy and fewer expensive special exhibitions, and a way of finally resolving the future prospects of the person on sick-leave. Drafting was made more difficult by the increasing hostility of those members of the committee who were also members of the museum syndicate. I was thankful for the support of the external members, who had no motive to whitewash what were some fairly glaring defects. In the end, though I suppose someone may have read the report, Jaffé became ill and soon resigned. It was understandably thought better to leave reforms to his successor; and in any case the university increasingly had other horrors to consider: student fees, cuts in government grants, quality assurance, and a slowly dawning realization of its own financial incompetence. A few suggested changes at the Fitzwilliam seemed insignificant compared with these wider issues.

There were, I suppose, some good things that came out of it, at least for me, if not for Cambridge as a whole. Apart from friendship with Jessica, there was my increased knowledge of the Fitzwilliam itself, and its wonderful contents; and the pleasure I used to get from leaving my car at St John's (by permission of the Master, a delightful ex-spy called Harry Hinsley, who had overlapped as Vice-Chancellor with Geoffrey in his longer stint as Vice-Chancellor at Oxford, and who was kindly disposed), and walking along to the museum, a part of Cambridge I otherwise seldom visited. I loved the feeling both of understanding more about how a museum and gallery worked, and of being properly part of Cambridge, for however short a time. And I suppose I also acquired a partial insight into the pitfalls that museums may fall into at the hands of an egocentric curator.

In October 1990 another impossible task came my way. I was asked by the Arts Council whether I would chair a committee to assess the management and financing of the Royal Opera House. This would involve first being a member of a panel to assess the Royal Opera (an assessment of the Royal Ballet had already been carried out), and then putting the two assessments together to make an overall report. This was all to start in 1991. I was in some difficulty, in that Geoffrey and I had both been asked to go to the United States for a semester in 1991, to an obscure university called Colman. I think we agreed to go as a kind of celebration of our now both being retired (I having left Girton at the end of September). Also we had only once been away together to a university abroad, and that was to Melbourne in 1985. We had enormously enjoyed that, but it had been only for six weeks, and we had had very specific lectures to give, and a good deal of free time.

This assignment would be very different. Though we had repeatedly asked exactly what we would be supposed to do if we went, and how much we would be paid, we had been able to extract no clear answer from Colman. We had had only a letter to say how delighted they were that we were coming. Geoffrey had far greater experience of American universities than I, and he was becoming concerned that they really did not have much idea what we would be supposed to do; and that we might end up standing in for people who were away, taking endless classes of first-year students and grading their papers. We both felt that, even for astronomical sums of money, we were too old for that. In any case, we asked ourselves, did we really want to be away, even together, for a whole semester? To which the answer was 'no'. I especially was looking forward to retirement, to settling down to work at home (having a series of lectures to write for the following spring), and getting down to serious gardening. So we wrote to say that after all we could not come. To which we had no reply of any kind. They must have been thankful.

At any rate this left me free to accept the poisoned chalice offered by the Arts Council, which became my worst entanglement with administration of the arts. The Royal Opera House was by now an embarrassment to the Arts Council, and they plainly wanted an independent committee to produce a report that would strengthen their determination to cut their grant to it, year on year. They were open to a great deal of hostile criticism for spending so much of the funds they received from the government on an organization which seemed manifestly to appeal only to a small minority; and even among that small minority who were interested in opera or ballet, only a few could afford the price of the tickets. Moreover, the Opera House itself was falling into disrepair, and was widely and correctly perceived as out-of-date, inadequate for the large number of performances that was mounted, and a danger to the audiences and those employed there. (A few years before, a stage-hand had been killed on stage when shifting scenery.)

The House was due to close for redevelopment in 1993. Morale was low, and the government under Mrs Thatcher was far from sympathetic towards either opera or ballet. In 1983 she had set up an independent inquiry into the management and finances of both the Royal Opera House and the Royal Shakespeare Company under Clive Priestley, a civil servant from the Cabinet Office, in response to increasing complaints of underfunding from both companies. This report recommended a substantial increase in funding for the Royal Opera House, on a permanent basis, keeping up with inflation. This was promised, but in the event the subsidy was paid for only one year, and then forgotten.

The Royal Opera House had three sources of funding: sales from tickets, government subsidy through the Arts Council and benefactions, corporate and individual, procured through the Royal Opera House Trust, a charity whose function was like that of the trustees of the Fitzwilliam Museum, but operating on a far grander scale. Corporate membership of the Trust could cost as much as £5,000 a year, and this along with various special fund-raising events brought in several millions each year. But none of these sources produced funds that were predictable, and opera had to be planned at least three years ahead, in order to book conductors and lead-singers. Ballet needed a shorter time, since most of the dancers were actually employed by the House. But showing opera and ballet in the same house (even though the Royal Ballet also had other venues, for example at Sadlers Wells) stretched resources dangerously, and was expensive, because the scene-shifters had to work in more than one team, continuously, which involved a great deal of overtime and unsocial hours pay.

In 1991, when the Arts Council committee was set up, Jeremy Isaacs had been in post as Director-General, in charge of both opera and ballet, since 1988. When appointed he had already been a member of the Covent Garden

Board, the body supposedly responsible for the Royal Opera House, and to which all employees, including the Director-General were responsible. He had worked in television for 30 years. His last job had been to establish and put on air the new ITV channel, Channel 4, which he had done with conspicuous and unhoped-for success. I had been a member of the IBA when we were allotted the frequency which enabled us to launch Channel 4, and we had had some doubts (or some of us had) about whether Jeremy Isaacs was the right person for the job. The trouble was that we did not know exactly what we wanted Channel 4 to be. We knew only that we wanted it to be different. The Act of Parliament that governed its content demanded that it should be innovative and experimental, as to both the form and content of programmes. But this meant little more than that it should not be simply more of the same. We knew Isaacs as an enormously energetic and imaginative producer and administrator in television; but we quite often disagreed with his judgement, had found him fearless, even ruthless, in defending himself against criticism, and more often than not proved right. But he was not a favourite among the timid. I was terrified at what we might see on the screen when Channel 4 opened; but it soon became clear that it had its own character and that it would be a success. This was a remarkable achievement.

We had had one dramatic dinner-party in Oxford, where we took Jeremy Isaacs and his wife Tamara to dine in Hall at Hertford to meet (at the request of both) my psychiatrist friend Philip Graham and his wife, also a psychiatrist. She had been greatly attached to Jeremy Isaacs as a student, but had left him in favour of Philip, and had not seen him since. Everything seemed to go well. I had not met either of the two wives before, and liked them both. But in the middle of dinner Philip's wife felt very ill, and I escorted her back to the Lodgings, where she recovered, but spent the rest of the evening talking to our youngest daughter, apparently most agreeably. I am sure her collapse was nothing to do with her reunion with Jeremy Isaacs. It could more plausibly be put down to the disgusting and excessive dinner.

Isaacs had always been ambitious. While he was still at Channel 4 Tamara died, and I suppose he was even more driven, and more unhappy than before. He hankered for new challenges. Indeed, he had no sooner been appointed to the Royal Opera House, and had not yet started work, than he applied to become Director-General of the BBC, after Alistair Milne had been sacked. Luckily he was not appointed. It is hard to imagine him at the BBC, and there would undoubtedly have been terrible rows. Instead, they appointed Michael Checkland, an accountant who had been their Head of Administration – an astonishingly different cup of tea.

This was a time when accountants and administrators were quite regularly appointed to posts which would earlier have gone to more creative people. Universities, colleges, museums, all hoped that someone who understood about money could help them through the hard times ahead. The Arts Council was no exception. The new chairman, Peter Palumbo, who had been appointed by Margaret Thatcher in 1990, himself appointed as secretary-general (the chief executive) one Anthony Everitt who had been deputy, and who as far as one could tell had no apparent interest in the arts whatsoever, but was determined to set targets and establish 'output criteria' and 'performance indicators', as the way to control and monitor expenditure. (Nothing, however, about, 'quality assurance', the concept beginning to bedevil the universities at this time.) By heroic fund-raising efforts, the Royal Opera House had broken even at the end of the 1980s, Jeremy Isaacs's bold insistence on exciting programming and high standards of performance filling almost all seats. But in the year 1991/92 it was once again facing a deficit of several millions, and was budgeting for a continuing and apparently ever larger deficit. Wages were rising, ticket sales declining. The orchestra had at one stage gone on strike, having demanded a 20 per cent pay increase, which could not possibly be afforded, and this was extremely expensive in box-office terms. It was such prospects that frightened the Arts Council into setting up its independent committee of appraisal, which I was to chair.

I went early in 1991 to meet some of the people involved in the opera appraisal panel. I was given minimal background papers, and had great difficulty in sorting out who was who, and where they came from. (I have always been hopelessly incompetent at listening to people's names when they introduce themselves, and I had no list of members to help me.). I was really floundering at this stage, but luckily was only a member of the panel, not its chairman. It was chaired by the secretary of the music panel of the Arts Council, Kenneth Baird. I knew something about the work and composition of this panel from my eldest son Felix, who had been a member of it for some years, but had recently resigned, on the grounds that he was running an orchestra, The Orchestra of the Age of Enlightenment, of which he had been a founder-member, and was in the process of applying to the Arts Council for funds. I quite liked Kenneth Baird at first. He was amiable and uncritical. But I gradually came to regard him as the epitome of all that was wet and wrong and indecisive about the Arts Council. He was obsessively tidy, a characteristic which, being so alien to me, I have never admired. He had dozens of pencils and pencil-sharpeners, and he spent most of our meetings sharpening the pencils and putting them to join the rank in his breast-pocket. I noted in my diary that this symbolized the ethos of the Arts Council – its inability to rise above the trivial.

At the beginning of May, I had three invitations to lunch, I imagine to soften me up. The first was with the Arts Council itself, where I was, I think quite improperly, given their views of the Royal Opera House. It was deeply unpopular. Their new secretary-general, Anthony Everitt, had recently commissioned a report entitled 'Towards a National Arts and Media Strategy', of which I was given a copy. The researchers had consulted every single organization who had applied for Arts Council funding over the last five years, and all were treated with equal respect, whether they were a group putting on street theatre in Wolverhampton or an internationally renowned lyric theatre. Various principles were enunciated, the chief of which was that London should not be given preferential treatment. It was impossible to extract any firm policy from the hugely expensive document. But generally I got the impression firstly that, if there had to be opera in London, the English National Opera was much to be preferred to Covent Garden, on the grounds that opera was performed by them in English. Secondly, that Jeremy Isaacs was a pain in the neck. Thirdly, that John Sainsbury, the chairman of the Board of Directors of Covent Garden, but about to resign, had been highly supportive of Jeremy Isaacs and was himself a great nuisance; things would certainly improve, I was told, when he had gone. I was astonished at the lack of discretion at this lunch-party: I was, after all, supposed to be chairing a neutral assessment committee.

My second lunch was a great deal more enjoyable. This was with Denis Forman, at his Granada Television office in Golden Square. He had been managing director of Granada from 1955 until 1988, and was still on their board. He had also been a director (member of the Board) of Covent Garden, and chairman of the opera board, one of the two subsidiary boards. I had known him from my days on the IBA, when he was at Granada. I had always greatly liked him. He was a soldierly Scot, of great imagination and with a passion for music. When *Brideshead* was being filmed in Oxford (and partly in Hertford College) in the 1970s we had seen quite a lot of him, and he had given a magnificent party in the Divinity Schools when the filming was over. At this lunch, without rancour or spite, he explained to me the vast expenses inevitably incurred in the running of an international opera house, and the financial difficulties that were to be expected, if the government would not give more money. I also learned for the first time about the plans for redevelopment during the closure time, still supposed to take place two years later.

The third lunch was with Peter Palumbo, in his magnificent office at the top of the Arts Council building in Great Peter Street. I learned little from this occasion, as he was interested in the visual arts but not in music or opera. He was a dapper little man, delighted to have become chairman of the Arts Council. We had an absolutely splendid lunch, brought up on trolleys, and accompanied by two different, superb white wines. I was mentally costing the whole thing. Apart from a generalized hostility to Isaacs, whom he clearly regarded as the loosest of loose cannons, I learned nothing new, except that he certainly was not about to risk offending Margaret Thatcher by supporting any plea for more money.

After this I was on my own. The assessment committee consisted of Brian Ivory, from the Scottish Arts Council, a whisky-distiller by profession; a City man called Dennis Stevenson, who was generally interested in the arts; Veronica Lewis, an expert on dance; Nigel Osborne, who was extremely left-wing, and, I think, a playwright and a believer in People's Theatre; and an enchanting German called Hans Landesmann, an opera director from one of the German city operas, whom my son Felix also knew and greatly liked. Sadly, duties in Germany prevented his staying with us to the end of our proceedings, and I greatly missed him, as a voice of tolerance and sanity, when he left. In his account of his time at the opera house, Jeremy Isaacs said that I knew nothing about ballet or opera.* This was not quite, but was nearly, true. I certainly had a great deal to learn about what it entailed to run an opera house, and put on performances of new opera or new productions of old opera, slotted in with performances of ballet.

We worked extremely hard all through June and July of 1991, meeting almost every day, and going round every corner of the Royal Opera House. We interviewed people from pretty well every side of the business; we saw all the senior staff more than once, but also talked to representatives of the backstage staff, the chorus, the orchestra and the people who ran the shop. We went about backstage, to see the costume rooms, the stored scenery and the rehearsal rooms. It was extraordinarily educative and absolutely terrifying. There were hundreds of old canvas sets of scenery, all of which could have got up in flames at the drop of a cigarette-end. There were people painting scenery, tucked away all by themselves behind the scenes, some of them apparently well into their eighties. We came upon one old man, painting away, of whom we asked what he was going to do when it came to closure (supposed to be two years ahead). He had never heard that there was going to be a

---

* Jeremy Isaacs, *Never Mind the Moon: My Time at the Royal Opera House* (London: Bantam Books, 1999).

closure. 'News to me', he said. Nobody we spoke to seemed to know how many people were employed on the premises, or how long they had been there, or what was in their contracts – if they had contracts. There was no retiring age, even for the chorus. (I had recently been to a pretty dire performance of *Orfeo ed Euridice* where it seemed that the chorus were on their last legs, and were pitilessly exposed to view.)

The orchestra, who had been on strike, were the most stroppy and discontent. Their spokesmen complained ceaselessly to us that they were paid less than other orchestral players and had no chance of earning extra money on the side. When I asked them why they did not leave, they had to admit that they liked working in London and not, like other orchestral players, having to undertake constant travel. They told us that they were the most important people in the House, and could prove it by the fact that when they went on strike there could be no performances. They, for the tax advantages it brought, were employed as freelance musicians, and therefore seemed to feel no solidarity with the aims of the House. They were a law to themselves. But the chorus also said that they were the most important people in the House, and had the worst time, because they perpetually had to learn new music, and new words, often in languages of which they knew nothing, and perform new movements. They hated the choreography involved in their work, and said that they sometimes felt they might as well be DANCERS.

I began to feel that anyone who was supposed to be in charge of all these people had a hopeless task. Jeremy Isaacs tried hard to get round and see everyone, especially when he was first appointed; but they all complained that they never knew what was happening, never knew what future plans there were, and apart from a certain pride in belonging to the Royal Opera House (all, that is, except the orchestral players), their morale seemed low. The real kings were the scenery men, who worked incredibly hard, always against the clock, to get new sets in place. They had a clear order of preference among operas, detesting, understandably, large lumpy sets, elaborate effects and frequent changes (with which I had some sympathy, from an aesthetic point of view).

The responsibilities of the sectional directors were highly confusing, to me at least. Taking opera and ballet together, there seemed to be vast numbers of people, the difference between whose spheres of authority I sometimes found it hard to grasp. The most challenging was the Director of Opera, Paul Findlay, with whom I immediately failed to get on. He described his main task as going round Europe picking productions of opera and ordering them for the Royal Opera House, some three years ahead. He seemed to have almost limitless powers. He had a wide knowledge of opera, of course, and a huge collection of recordings, but he was not a professional musician. I thought that he was extremely lucky to have the job. He had read Greats at Oxford, and attached himself to me, because he knew I was a philosopher. He asked me, early on, whether I had known his father, J. N. Findlay, a notable Hegelian scholar in the University of London, and a notoriously bad-tempered man. Paul asked me what I thought of him. I was hard put to it to answer, because at that moment all I could think of was that when he used to come to Oxford in the 1950s it was widely reported that he was in love with our friend and colleague David Pears, and that he used to come out in a rash whenever David entered the room. I did not think that this would do as a comment.

Very early on in our interviewing timetable, Paul Findlay said that he wanted to get out of what he referred to as 'this place', and was looking for another job. (I was vividly reminded of the manner in which my children, when discontented with the contents of the refrigerator, used always to say, 'Why is there never any bacon/ice cream/lemonade [or whatever it was] in This House?') I don't think that Findlay's desire to leave was generally known. He was, in fact, eased out two years later, and replaced by Nicholas Payne, a far calmer character and a better musician.

As our work proceeded, tempers got pretty short among the staff. They had plenty to do without our constantly demanding to see them again. There was one day in July, for example, when we saw Jeremy Isaacs for about three hours. We could not stop him; he simply ranted on about how government must produce more money. We were trying, by now, to get him to talk coherently about the coming closure, or rather the redevelopment of the site while the House was closed for refurbishment, and what he planned to do with the companies when the theatre was closed. The plan was both to make the existing theatre a safer and more spacious place to work in, to install modern machinery to work the curtains and enable scenes to be shifted, to enlarge the outlying parts of the building, for example, the crush hall and catering area, but also to put up a large office block, the rents from which would finance the enormous costs of refurbishment and enlargement. What the companies would actually do during the time that all this took was not yet clear. However, the need for the redesign of the House was of immediate urgency. We had talked to the health and safety officers of Westminster Council, who said that they could close the House any day, if they came round and did a proper inspection, which they had postponed, because they knew that closure was imminent. The paradox was that the council steadfastly refused to give planning permission for the new office block which was an essential part of the plan.

207

Without it, it seemed that there would be no way of generating the money. It was the kind of frustrating, enraging situation which would have caused anyone, even someone less given to bursts of temper than Isaacs, to ranting fury.

It was not an enjoyable time. The chaotic management, the permanent shortage of cash, the lack of clarity about redevelopment, combined with Isaacs's determination that nothing must stand in the way of new opera and new ballet, even if it could not be expected to be a box-office success, all led to head-spinning despair, at least on my part. And members of the appraisal committee were beset by endless literature from a pressure group called the Covent Garden Community Association, who hated the Opera House, and constantly blocked its expansion and redevelopment by placing objections with Westminster Council, which the latter was bound, I suppose, to take note of. I think I wrote to this organization five times refusing to meet them. They were nothing if not persistent. If I, only briefly connected with the Opera House, suffered such persecution, I dread to think what the directors and members of staff must have put up with. The force behind this pressure group was someone called Jim Monahan, an architect who, according to Jeremy Isaacs, was motivated by not having won the competition to design the redeveloped Opera House, and was determined to have his revenge.*

There was manifestly neither the money nor the necessary planning permissions for closure and redevelopment to start, as scheduled, in 1993. We, the appraisal committee, felt certain that the money would not be forthcoming from government. I made an appointment to see David Mellor, the Secretary of State for the National Heritage, and I turned

---

* See Jeremy Isaacs, *Never Mind the Moon*, p. 206.

up to meet him on the very day that he was clearing his desk, having been forced to resign because of the sex scandal which ended his political career. I had got to know him quite well in his Home Office days in the 1980s, when I was chairman of the Home Office Advisory Committee on Animal Experiments. I had liked him; he was clever, quick to see a point and possessed of an attractive perkiness that appealed to me, especially in contrast with the pomposities of the Home Office. He greeted me warmly on this occasion, thankful, as he said, to talk about something other than the scandal that had engulfed him (but by which he did not seem to be unduly put out). He had absolutely no hope to offer. I realized of course that he was the lamest possible duck and had lost whatever interest he had had; and that he had little to say in favour of Jeremy Isaacs.

I had a less frivolous conversation with Hayden Phillips, a permanent secretary at the department. He took time to go through all the possible options for the Opera House, including building a new theatre, or moving to another. I liked him very much indeed, and thought that he was full of genuine goodwill; but of course he was powerless to get Mrs Thatcher to move from her implacable hostility to the Royal Opera House. It stood for everything that she most hated. She thought its Board members, or directors, were snobbish intellectuals, many of them from Oxford (which she had reason to dislike, since the university had genuinely insulted her by refusing her an honorary degree – an honour which up to that time every prime minister who was an alumnus had received). Moreover, the fact that Isaacs had been conspicuously successful in television did not endear him to her; she loathed and despised all television companies indifferently, believing them to conspire against her, refusing to recognize her unique genius. There was absolutely no one at the House who was 'one of us'. So, knowing all this, I came away very despondent.

Meanwhile, one of our number, Dennis Stevenson, had been studying the redevelopment plans, including their financial aspect, and had concluded, unsurprisingly, that without a huge capital grant they were unworkable. And there was to be no huge capital grant. Moreover, the great office block that was to finance the rest looked more and more dubious as a source of funding. There were too many empty office blocks in central London at this time. I had one last meeting with Jeremy Isaacs to try to persuade him, temporarily and while the debts were so enormous, to cut down on new productions at the Opera House, and try to sell more tickets by putting on more performances that would be certain to sell out, not necessarily because of big-name singers, but because of the popularity of the operas themselves, *Rigoletto, Traviata, Don Giovanni,* and so on. He was understandably imitated by such a philistine suggestion. Being a world-class opera house entailed putting on new productions, even if they had been picked up somewhat at random.

We wrote our report in August and it was published in September 1991. It recommended various changes in management, including the employment of an extra member of staff in the personnel department to try to improve communications among the employees. We urged closure sooner rather than later, on the grounds that the stage and backstage were simply not safe and the fire-hazards were horrendous. And we suggested that since there was manifestly not enough money for the grand redevelopment, and none was forthcoming, it should be dropped and only refurbishment embarked on, wasteful of money though this might be in the long term. Finally we suggested that new productions should be limited for the foreseeable future to not more than four a year; and that only the wing of the ballet based in Birmingham (the Birmingham Royal Ballet) should go on tour, not the Royal Ballet proper. We were pretty critical of the management as a whole, and even more critical of the Board of the Royal Opera House, who seemed to us unprofessional and unprepared to give enough time or to take enough responsibility. There had been a tradition of Board membership consisting of opera-lovers and balleto-manes, who had rejoiced in the kudos attached to membership, and to the free tickets to which they were entitled, but who were, many of them, pretty ignorant of the real troubles of the House. Things had improved, it is true, in recent years, John Sainsbury having insisted on a limited term of office as a director. But Sainsbury had resigned, and the air of amateurishness among some of the members remained. So our report was fairly sharp in tone. But it was intended to be helpful and constructive; it was also intended to make clear without any doubt how desperately the Royal Opera House needed proper Arts Council funding (government funding, that is) if it were to survive as an international lyric theatre. Someone leaked a story to the press which made the report sound even more negative than it was. Poor Jeremy Isaacs saw this press story while he was abroad, and before he had seen the report, and was extremely angry. (We did not in fact blame him for the managerial shortcomings we found, still less for the financial horrors. We held that ultimately the directors must take responsibility.)

I, with my fellow-members of the committee, presented the report in September to the Arts Council, who had commissioned it, and this was a bland and characteristically tedious occasion, though we pointed out both that our report had been unanimous (indeed we had almost no internal disagreements, even with the believer in People's Theatre) and that we did not lay the blame on Jeremy Isaacs but on what, on that occasion and orally, we described as the weakness of the Board, and the weakness and indecisiveness of the members of the Arts Council themselves. They seemed not to hear this.

Then I was asked whether I would present the report to the Board of the Royal Opera House. I had not been warned of this, and I was reluctant to do it, not only because I thought it would be painful, but because I was short of time. In any case, I had not thought that it would be part of my duties to do this, believing (I still think correctly) that the Arts Council themselves should present it. It was after all a report commissioned by and addressed to them.

I had arranged to go back to Wiltshire after the meeting with the Arts Council. However, I was told that the Board of the Opera House had convened a meeting in the afternoon, to which I was bidden. No one else was invited to attend. I rang up Angus Stirling, now chairman of the Board of the House, who had been very courteous to us when we had talked to him, but who seemed to me out of his depth, and certainly an exemplification of the semi-detached attitude of the Board, since he was also chairman of the National Trust, and was fairly distrait. I asked him how long he thought I should allow for the presentation of the report, and told him that I had another engagement to which I was committed, out of London. He said he thought I should allow about a quarter of an hour. So I rang up Geoffrey and told him when I would be back.

I arrived and stood in the passage for about twenty minutes, and then was invited in. I made a short presentation, as politely as I could, and then Angus Stirling said, 'Thank you. Now I will go round the table and ask each director in turn to ask questions.' I was dumbfounded. I don't know how many members of the Board there were, but I am certain there were no absentees. Of course the questions were uniformly hostile; and of course, as is always the case, it was assumed that I had put the report together single-handed. In my replies I was careful to speak always of 'the committee' or 'my colleagues and I'. I felt a profound longing for some support in this appalling grilling; but above all I was anxious about the time it was taking.

After an hour, when we had got only halfway round the table, I asked whether I might break off to go and telephone my husband who was expecting me home. I was permitted to leave, but no one offered to find me a telephone, and in fact I could not find one. I thought I was wasting more time looking, and also probably further enraging the Board. So I hastened back to my seat in the stocks. The whole proceedings took two and a half hours, and all I could do was to give the shortest possible answers and try not to look at my watch too blatantly. I was asked repeatedly to substantiate our charges of inefficient management, to which I could only refer them to the pages of the report. I was asked whether I did not realize that refurbishing the House and rewiring it would enforce closure any way, and that therefore the full redevelopment ought to be done at the same time, in reply to which I could only ask where the money was to come from. Finally I was attacked for not having called attention to the excellence of productions both in ballet and opera in recent years. To which I replied that we had been concerned with management and finance, not with aesthetic judgements, a reply that I regretted, because it both obscured the fact that we had largely sympathized with Jeremy Isaacs' desire to see the Royal Opera House among the great opera houses of the world, and made us seem indifferent to the plain fact that management and finance were both meant to serve excellence in performance. However, I noted later that in his book, Isaacs wrote, 'To mix criticism with sermons on management muddles both.'* And I suppose this was partly what I thought. One way and another, it was one of the worst afternoons that I remember, and I left at last feeling a complete idiot, and that I should not have been subjected to such bullying without warning. It was worse than Jaffé.

I do not know whether our report made any difference or not. Probably the changes that began to be made had already been thought of or had been suggested by Price Waterhouse (who were carrying out an audit commissioned by the Royal Opera House Board), as well as by us. But it is true that the deficit was gradually reduced. One thing at least followed the publication of the report, and that was that the government at last recognized that the redevelopment of the Opera House was urgent, and undertook to contribute money. But I doubt if our report was influential in this. John Major had by now succeeded Mrs Thatcher as prime minister, and he shared none of her prejudices. Most beneficial of all was his introduction of the National Lottery, which Mrs Thatcher had always refused to countenance; and the Royal Opera House put in a bid in 1995. Closure and redevelopment at last began in 1997, when Jeremy Isaacs's term of office ended. Now, in 2002, after many dramas and disasters, the Royal Opera House appears to be flourishing, with a new musical director and a new general director, having made a modest profit for two years in succession.

The fearful meeting with the Board of the Royal Opera House was my last contact, either with the management of

---

* Jeremy Isaacs, *Never Mind the Moon*, p. 276.

the House or with the Arts Council. However, a few years later I found myself thinking again about the issues of government sponsorship of the arts and the arguments that had led up to that encounter, though thankfully this time from a theoretical rather than a practical standpoint.

As a millennium enterprise a charitable body called Peer (whose main functions I never quite discovered, but which was concerned mostly with the encouragement of the visual arts) decided to publish a compilation of essays, drawings and poems, which would explore sponsorship and administration of the arts in this country at the beginning of the new century. I was asked to be one of two editors, who would select the material submitted and each contribute an introduction. My fellow-editor was to be Mark Wallinger, of whom I had never heard until then, but whose work I came to love: original, bold and above all funny. He has a passion for horses, and once submitted his horse as an exhibit. She was a racehorse, sadly anything but successful. Horses were never far from the inspiration of his work.

In order to discuss the project, and find out whether it was something I could possibly do, I invited Andrew Brighton, a painter who was a trustee of Peer (and who had taught my youngest daughter at her art college), and their curatorial director, Ingrid Svenson, and Mark Wallinger to discuss the project in the House of Lords. I instantly liked all of them, and we had an extremely jolly and, it seemed, fruitful meeting, during which I discovered that Mark and his girl-friend lived in a flat at the top of the building in Camberwell where I share a flat with my youngest daughter. It was such an absurd coincidence that it quite made up my mind to accept the commission, and the volume came out in the autumn of 2000, under the title *Art for All: Their Policies and our Culture*, published by the Peer Foundation.

We had enormous fun going through the numerous submissions for the volume; we met frequently, and Ingrid worked extremely hard and with great efficiency, rejecting the impossible, and sending us to read what still amounted to a huge number of possible pieces for inclusion. I was very keen that we should include some historical documents, to put the current position of arts administration in the context of 1945, when the Arts Council was born. This was done, and the last section of the book is essential reading for an understanding of the difficulties, which I believe to be insoluble, of any attempt to implement a coherent general policy for the arts. Right from Maynard Keynes's first statement of the principles of the Arts Council it was plain that there was an inbuilt contradiction. The first necessity, he argued, was to 'rebuild our common life'; and this would mean the repair and erection of galleries, concert halls and theatres all over the country. But he gave equal priority to plans for London, to make it a great international 'artistic metropolis'; and this essentially entailed reopening the Royal Opera House and establishing a National Theatre. As one decade followed another, the conflict of interest between London and 'the regions' became sharper, as our extracts from Arts Council reports plainly show. Hidden within this conflict, however, was another, even more profound. What are 'the arts'?

Raymond Williams, in an article published in the *Political Quarterly* in 1979, pointed out that, under its first charter in 1946, the Arts Council was concerned with 'fine arts exclusively'. The 'fine arts' were held to be easily identifiable; and what was good or bad within that category equally easily discerned. Maynard Keynes, after all, though he mentioned innovation and creativity, could nevertheless speak with confidence about art in its 'noblest forms', certain that these forms could be discerned, and separated from

216

what was ignoble. At its inception, the Arts Council had been directly under the Treasury. Its function was to exercise its own judgement in the distribution of Treasury funds. It was of all bodies (with the possible exception of the governors of the BBC) the most obviously made up of 'the Great and the Good' whose taste generally dictated what was fine art and what was not, and what was good or bad within the category of fine art. But the very 'socialization' that Keynes had repudiated had brought about immense changes since 1945. Radio and television had transformed and democratized the idea of art. And, while Keynes believed that the aesthetic was a realm apart, quite separate from politics, increasingly such a view came to be regarded as itself political, the voice of an old-fashioned ruling class. From the left came echoes of the arts policies of the Soviet Union, where evaluation of the worth of the arts was explicitly social and political. The doctrine of *Narodnost*, or Art for the People, reflected an aspiration to a better life for all the people. In Tony Blair's introduction to the Labour Party manifesto of 1997, he spoke of the party's belief in strong communities, 'with shared values, and the equal worth of all, with no one cast aside'. Chris Smith, Secretary of State for Culture Media and Sport in Blair's first government, was even more explicit. In his book of essays, *Creative Britain*,* he wrote 'perhaps most important is that the arts are for everyone. Things of quality must be available to the many, not just the few. Cultural activity is not some elitist exercise that takes place in reverential temples aimed at the predelictions of the cognoscenti.'

Thus the word 'elitist' has, since 1997, been formally introduced into the debate. Of all the words in the political vocabulary, it is the most noxious. The opposite of 'elitist' is

---

* Chris Smith, *Creative Britain* (London: Faber & Faber, 1998).

of course 'accessible'; and this has come to mean not so much what it is physically or financially possible for people to get to, to watch or listen to or look at, as what they will find it easy to watch or listen to or look at, what they will immediately prefer and spontaneously engage with, without trouble. It is connected in sense with the concept of the inclusive, itself a highly politically correct notion, calling attention above all to the shared values to which Tony Blair referred in the 1997 manifesto. This cluster of ideas between them rules out altogether the old notion of 'high culture', or 'fine art' on which the Arts Council and government arts policy was founded. And there are many who will say 'Quite right, too.' But there is a profound difference between the goal of enabling people to enjoy and understand the best in the arts, and the assumption that what is best is what the majority of people want or already understand. This difference has not been noticed by the present government.

There is a parallel ambiguity in the governmental attitude to the universities, where it is just as damaging. Here the notions of social class and academic ability are most openly confused. No one wants to exclude those of any social class from university education; but no one wants to offer university education to those with neither interest nor ability to pursue it. (That there is a link between academic interest and social class is statistically true; but it is not a causal nor a necessary connection.) The 'elite', in the case of the universities, are the academically inclined; in the case of the arts, they are people of knowledge and taste, who can distinguish the good from the trivial.

The aim of 'accessibility' ought to come second, subordinate to the aim of high standards, whether in the academic or the artistic world. The fate of recorded music is a sad illustration of what happens when accessibility is put first.

218

Classic FM, the enormously popular radio station specializing in broadly defined classical music, was intended to introduce a wide audience to what was hitherto thought of as an elitist preserve. But in the nature of the case it had to deal in short pieces, or single movements from longer works, its balance of words and music having been geared to a relatively short attention span, and advertisments having to be accommodated, as well as breaks for news and travel updates. In consequence the taste for whole symphonies, long choral works, new music or music demanding close attention has markedly declined. Records now are almost all old recordings used on air of music popularized by Classic FM, which provides what is essentially background music, often described as 'relaxing'. So far from introducing a new audience to music that is either new, or new to them, the effect of the popularity of Classic FM has been to feed its faithful audience with a species of easy listening, issued either on air or as spin-off CDs.

As long as standards remain high, and imagination is not stifled, then everything can and should be done to enable people who want to to enjoy the arts and benefit from them. After all, there could hardly be any public performances more accessible than the Proms. It is true that not everyone wants to attend them, or listen to them on the radio. But for those who do, there is absolutely nothing to stop them; and the Proms, over the years, have contributed vastly to 'high culture', just as scholarships for the poor to Oxford or Cambridge have contributed vastly to learning and research. Such a subordinate aim is miles remote from the present aims of the Arts Council and of the government, where if something is not enjoyed by everyone it is morally tainted, divisive, 'exclusive', and not fit for the new century. I picked up some leaflets from the Arts Council headquarters as I was walking past a few months ago. One of them started with a list of 'Our Priorities'. The first was 'Bringing the arts to a wider audience'; the second, 'Encouraging individuality and experimentation'; the third, 'Nurturing creativity'; the fourth, 'Embracing the diversity of our culture'; the fifth, and last, 'Exploring new forms of experience'. One would have hoped for some reference to standards of excellence in the creative and performing arts. That must be left now to those fortunate enough to get money from the National Lottery: but the wider the ethos of accessibility spreads, the less likely it is, say, that the Royal Opera House or the more specialist orchestras will win funds.

We are facing a future where, if we are not careful, just as children from independent schools who have been well educated will be debarred from university places, so those of us with informed, not necessarily conservative, tastes will not have our artistic needs provided for, on grounds of pure prejudice. In his autobiographical (and extremely funny) book, *Tainted by Experience*, John Drummond, former director of the Edinburgh Festival, writes, 'Failing to differentiate between the good and the indifferent while sheltering under a cloud of spurious democracy is not good enough. It is a betrayal of all that our civilization has stood for.'* With this I profoundly agree. Nor will I be shaken by the derisive questions, 'Who are you to set up a standard of taste? How can you tell the good from the indifferent?' There are two ways: one is by education, by constantly looking, listening, reading. Education gets your eye in, if you are really interested. And an educated person can teach you to see or hear excellence where you might not have recog-

---

* John Drummond, *Tainted by Experience: A Life in the Arts* (London: Faber & Faber, 2000).

nized it by yourself. The second way is more primitive: it is the shiver that goes down your spine (or, in my case, down my legs) when I read something, new or familiar, that is really poetry, or when I hear something, new or familiar, performed with an authentic spark.

This second way was the answer that A. E. Housman gave to the question 'How do you know that something is poetry?', in his lecture, 'The Name and Nature of Poetry.'* At the end of his lecture he quoted a poem by Blake, and said, 'I am not equal to framing definite ideas which would match the magnificent versification and correspond to the strong tremor of unreasonable excitement which those words set up in some region deeper than the mind.'

And finally he quotes one more stanza:

> Tho' thou art worship'd by the names divine
> Of Jesus and Jehovah, thou art still
> The Son of Morn in weary Night's decline
> The lost traveller's dream under the hill.

Commenting on this, he said, 'It purports to be theology; what theological sense, if any, it may have, I cannot imagine and feel no wish to learn: it is pure and self-existent poetry which leaves no room in me for anything else.'

I, for my part, do not believe that we should be compelled to deny our human ability to respond, physically as well as mentally, to what is truly art. Without confidence in this ability, in others as well as ourselves, we are faced with the death of art.

---

* A. E. Housman, 'The Name and Nature of Poetry', Leslie Stephen Lecture, 1933, repr. in John Carter (ed.), Selected Prose (Cambridge: Cambridge University Press, 1961).

# Index

Adrian, Richard 156, 161
Alton, Lord 137
Anisuddin, Mr 84
Antinori, Professor 140
Aquinas, Thomas 71, 95
Archer, Mary 190
Aristotle 16, 17
Augustus 182
Austin, J. L. 107

Baird, Kenneth 201–2
Baker, Kenneth 65–6
Barnes, Dame Josephine 78, 104–5, 106
Beckett, Margaret 61
Bentham, Jeremy 169–70, 173, 174
Blair, Tony 29, 164, 169, 217
Bowra, Maurice 186
Brighton, Andrew 215
Britten, Sir Ted 47–8, 49–50, 53, 54, 68
Broad, C. D. 148
Bush, George 141

Carriline, Madeline 89, 90
Checkland, Michael 200
Chorlton, Mr 184
Clothier, Sir Cecil 127, 129
Cockerell, C. R. 189
Coe, Richard 2–3
Cooke, George 36–7

Cooper, Jack 183–4
Copernicus 149
Crane, Mr Justice 139–40
Croft, Jenny 77, 80, 85, 98, 108
Cross, Lord 150, 153
Cross, Venetia 150

Davies, Dr David 104, 113
Dawes, Geoffrey 83
Dawes, Margaret 83
Deech, Ruth 125
Donaldson, Sir Liam 136
Drummond, John 220
Dunstan, Gordon 156, 157, 158–60
Dyson, Anthony 89

Eccles, Lady 176
Ede, Chuter 32–3
Edwards, Dr 73, 74
Elias, Thomas 177
Everitt, Anthony 200, 202

Faithful, Lucy 31–2, 56
Findlay, J. N. 206
Findlay, Paul 206
Fish, John 41–2, 58
Fitzwilliam, Lord 189
Ford, Dr Norman 95, 96
Forman, Denis 202–3
Forrester, Sam 59, 60
Fowler, Norman 74, 76, 81, 110

# Index

Galton, David 97
Genochio, Miss 8
Graham, Philip 40–1, 42–3, 48, 54, 57, 60, 199
Green, Henry 3–4
Greengross, Dr Wendy 104

Habgood, Dr John 120
Halstead, Michael 189–90
Harries, Bishop Richard 138
Hedger, John 31, 45
Hinsley, Harry 195–6
Houghton, Lord 123, 124, 125
Housman, A. E. 221
Huxley, Aldous 134

Isaacs, Jeremy 198–200, 201, 202, 203, 204, 205, 207–8, 209, 210, 211–12, 213–14
Ivory, Brian 203

Jaffé, Michael 191–4, 195, 214
Johnson, Dr 23

Keynes, Maynard 181–2, 216–17
Kogan, Maurice 5
Kornberg, Hans 19–20, 21

Lander, Eric 128–9
Landesmann, Hans 204
Lewis, Veronica 203
Lloyd, Jane 160
Lockwood, Michael 98
Longford, Frank 76, 93
Luxton, Imogen 45–6, 58, 67
Lynam, Elizabeth 106

Mahoney, Father 88
Major, John 215
Marshall, John 92–3, 108
Matheson, John 187
Matheson, Muir 187
Maud, Jean 185–6
Maud, John 186
Maxwell, Robert 34

McKay, Lord 119
McKie, Robin 114
McLaren, Dr Anne 81–6, 94, 110, 112–3
McNaughton, Callum 107, 110
Mellor, David 161, 162, 208–9
Metters, Jeremy 76–7, 80, 81, 106, 108
Mill, John Stuart 180–1
Milne, Alistair 200
Mittler, Professor Peter 44, 66–7
Monahan, Jim 208
Monteverdi 18
Morton, John 24

Nietzsche 43
Nodder, Mr 76

Onslow, Earl of 176
Orwell, George 134
Osborne, Nigel 203

Page, Robin 24
Palumbo, Peter 200, 203
Paton, Bill 160
Payne, Nicholas 207
Pears, David 206–7
Peers, Jack 183–4, 185
Phillips, Hayden 209
Pilkington, Constance 184–5, 186, 187–8
Plato 43
Plowden, Bridget 4
Porter, Hal 3
Powell, Enoch 116–17
Priestly, Clive 198
Priestly, Peter 41–2

Quinton, Mrs 101

Ramsbotham, David 101
Rankin, Chief Inspector 161
Rawnsley, Ken 80, 106, 107, 108, 110
Rawson, Dame Jessica 191, 194, 195

# Index

Robertson, David  9
Rose, Bernard  186
Rousseau  23

Sainsbury, John  202, 211
Schuster, Felix  195
Segal, Stan  34
Sewell, Anna  153
Singer, Peter  115, 169–73
Smith, Chris  217
Smith, Lord (of Guildford)  175
Soulsby, Lord  176
Southwood, Dick  19–20
St John Stevas, Norman  109
Stefansson, Kari  144, 145, 146
Steptoe, Mr  73, 74
Stevens, Vivien  46, 61
Stevenson, Dennis  203, 210
Stirling, Angus  212
Stock, Professor Gregory  128–9, 141
Stuart, H. G.  16
Svenson, Ingrid  215

Thatcher, Margaret  29, 197–8, 200, 203, 209, 214
Thucydides  4
Tumim, Stephen  39, 101
Tumim, Winifred  39–40, 49

Venter, Craig  128, 134
Virgil  182

Walker, Jean  80, 103–4, 105
Walker, Michael  31, 46, 47
Walker, Micheline  31
Waller, Rabbi  115
Wallinger, Mark  215
Walton, Lord John  120–1
Warnock, Felix  157, 201, 204
Warnock, Geoffrey  5–6, 7, 9, 12, 28, 62, 63, 73, 75, 83, 87, 109, 110, 115–16, 157, 191, 192, 196, 212
Warnock, Kitty  157
Waton, Lord  138
Whewell, William  189
White, Christopher  191
Wiggins, David  24
Wigley, Dafydd  117–18
Wilking, Virginia  42
Wilkinson, Frank  7
Williams, Bernard  162
Williams, David  162
Williams, Philip  58
Williams, Raymond  216
Williams, Shirley  62–3
Winkley, David  18–19
Wordsworth  23, 180–1

Yellowlees, Sir Henry  81
York, Archbishop of  121